# Women in Design
a contemporary view

# Women in Design

## a contemporary view

Liz McQuiston

RIZZOLI
NEW YORK

First published in the United States of America in 1988
by Rizzoli International Publications, Inc.
597 Fifth Avenue, New York, NY 10017

*To Nellie Glass McQuiston*

Library of Congress Cataloging-in-Publication Data

McQuiston, Liz.
  Women in design.

  Includes bibliographical references.
  1. Women designers — History — 20th century.
I. Title.
NK1174.M36 1988      745.4'088042      87-63254
ISBN 0-8478-0944-7 (pbk.)

Book/cover design: Liz McQuiston

Origination of illustrations by Scantrans, Singapore
Set in Plantin by Goodfellow and Egan Ltd.,
Cambridge, England
Printed and bound in Italy by Graphicom SRL

# Contents

# Introduction

The profile of the design profession has changed significantly over the past five to ten years. The presence of women is now becoming apparent at all levels and, to varying degrees, in all the separate disciplines. This book is intended to be a celebration of that change, and evidence of the variety of ways in which women are contributing to the design field internationally, whether working in teams, in partnership with other men or women, or working solo.

Taking graphic design in Britain for example: women designers are now fairly common in studios, and graphic design courses in colleges and polytechnics can expect roughly 50% of their student intake to be women – a very different picture from even five years ago. This is all to the good. One can't help but feel that it is important to have women involved in a profession which, in its many guises, is responsible for communicating the majority of information that instructs, persuades, educates and entertains us in everyday life. Especially as roughly half the receivers are women. Having said that, however, it is only recently that women have been actively employed in many areas of design education in positions of leadership. Courses in textiles and fashion were traditionally led by women, but in the early 1980s there were still few (if any) women heading courses or departments in other design areas.

Changes in America seem to have been much more dramatic. An article on women designers in *ID Magazine* in 1986 states: 'According to the US Department of Labor Statistics, the percentage of female designers (defined as all designers but architects) jumped from 25% to 52% nationwide during the years 1980 to 1985.'[1] This is quite startling, considering that the statement refers to *all* designers but architects and also considering the very size of the American industries involved.

Whether one is speaking of America's progressive leaps or Britain's slow but steady road to change, there is definitely a shift underway. The socio-economic background to this shift is best explained by historians, social scientists and writers of feminist theory. As a designer and educator, my interest lies in recording and furthering the changes that are taking place, and providing hope and encouragement to my students. There *is* cause for celebration . . . there are also a lot of set-backs and difficulties in day-to-day working relationships to be sorted out along the way.

Certain problems arise in discussing the subject of women in design, beginning with the phrase itself. Many women in the design field want to be acknowledged for the ideas and work they produce, as opposed to being singled out for the fact that they happen to be women. This is a highly admirable principle – it is also a surefire path to obscurity, especially as we are talking about a field that is highly competitive and heavily based on promotion. On the whole, men welcome any opportunity to broadcast their achievements, while women seem more inclined to avoid potential ego clashes and melt into the crowd. Any excuse to push them into the spotlight is acceptable in my opinion. Why not?

At the same time, there is a separatist view to be avoided ie. the suggestion of two opposing sides: women in design versus men in design. Generally speaking, unless fairly obvious clues are present it is extremely difficult, if not impossible, to take any given design (graphic or product) and determine whether its creator was a man or a woman. The gender of the designer is rarely an issue in design criticism. Visual qualities don't fall into a male or female bracket either. Making such distinctions in terms of an end product is to my mind very difficult ground. Where differences and distinctions *can* emerge is in the nature of the design process itself – for example, in establishing a design approach, interpreting the needs or requirements of the user, assigning priorities with regard to function or appearance, and in the activity of decision-making or negotiating in teamwork. Women apply a different psychological framework and life experience (ie. viewpoint) to design decision-making. This should be welcomed and recognised as a positive contribution in determining the nature of a product or message conveyed – it should not be reduced to superficial issues such as men like hard edges and women prefer curves. Surely our visions of designing for the future should incorporate both male and female viewpoints.

Moving on to more specific points about this book . . . its main emphasis is on women designers active in the profession today, although there are a few included who are now retired and one who is no longer alive (Marie Neurath died in 1986). The designers involved are a mixed bag: some have international reputations; some are influential and known within their own design area; some undertake challenging problems or produce innovative work but are relatively unknown. All however are (or were) breaking ground or making an impact on the profession, whether through education or practice, or both. It must also be said that they are not a definitive collection; there are many more like them operating all over the world but it is impossible to include them all in one book. A selection was made which attempts to achieve a balanced mix of different design areas *and* different ages.

As to the design areas covered: women and their design work have been publicised in some areas, such as the decorative arts or crafts, and almost ignored in others. This book concentrates on design areas not traditionally associated with women, for example graphic design, industrial design, environmental design and architecture. This does not suggest that harsh boundaries have been drawn and other areas excluded as such. It simply means that one tried to avoid entrenchment in areas where women already receive heavy coverage, such as illustration, textiles, fashion, etc. Nevertheless, the outline on which the collection of designers was based still seems fairly broad. It was as follows:

Graphic design, television and computer graphics, advertising, animation, audio visual, video;
Industrial design, product design, furniture design;
Architecture, interior design;
Exhibition design, television/film production design;
Design management, education, history and research

In the end, a compilation of this nature can only offer an introduction to the subject. Like any sourcebook, it does not provide information in-depth, but entices the reader on to further exploration of the people and work contained. I view it as one of many steps to be taken to encourage and promote women working in design; hopefully it will also open the reader's eyes (as it has mine) to work being conducted across a variety of design disciplines. The 1980s promises to be the decade in which design is finally recognised as a crucial activity in determining our quality of life and our future social development; it also promises to be the decade in which the contribution of women to the design activity will be consolidated.

Liz McQuiston
London, February 1988

[1]Lisa Krohn, 'Against the Odds: five top designers discuss the challenges unique to women in design', *ID Magazine*, New York, September/October 1986, pp38–43.

# Notes and acknowledgements

As stated in the introduction ( and it can't be said often enough) this book is *not* intended to be a definitive collection of any sort; it is an exploratory view of work by contemporary women designers, and I hope that there will be many more projects of this nature to come. I say that with even greater conviction now than when I started. For once I began contacting designers in various countries and collecting new names from discussions that evolved, it became obvious, all too quickly, that my efforts were only going to be able to touch the tip of the iceberg. I would have liked to pursue designers in Spain, Scandinavia, South America, etc – but that will have to wait for another project. Also there are particular designers I was keen to include – Gae Aulenti of Italy, Ray Eames of the USA, for example – but for one reason or another, could not.

But there it is . . . and it must be said that the time constraints were quite deadly. Initial letters were sent to about half the designers at the end of August 1987, and the others were approached as time went on. The contributions were collected via the post over four months, from September to December – an altogether hair-raising affair. The Italian post lost half the material I put into it; there were also problems in travelling from the reverse direction. But despite accidents and many necessarily brief and disjointed conversations by telephone, it all arrived in one place in the end. I have to thank all the designers in this book who combatted such difficulties, and their own hectic schedules, to produce material with such speed.

I am also grateful to many people who offered advice and moral support during the compilation of this book. Some of them are listed here; those who are not still have my thanks and I hope will forgive the lack of mention, purely a product of the blank state of mind that sets in at the end of a long haul.

But there are two people I would like to give special thanks: one is Henri Henrion, a dear friend for ten years now, who offered help in the way of contacts during my initial research, and encouragement every step of the way. As a designer (and personality) of truly international status, Henrion has done more than anyone to put designers from different countries in touch with each other, both professional and student alike (we all often grumble, but he perseveres). I thank him for teaching me to always think of myself as part of an international design community – a principle which had great influence on the formulation of this book.

Last but by no means least: I owe a great deal (far more than she realises) to Julia King, who joined the project in its last stages to help with the design. It was Julia who supplied the final surge of fire and enthusiasm, picked it all up and threw it back on the drawing board – long after my energy had run out.

LMcQ

Many thanks are due to the following for lending
help, hard work, or advice to this project:

FHK Henrion
Julia King
Pauline Carter
Micki Hawkes/ Architectural Association
Irene Kotlarz/ Bristol Festival of Animation
Richard Taylor/Royal College of Art
Peter Wheeler
Nigel Coates/Branson Coates
Sy Chen/Creative Intelligence Associates/Tokyo
Naomi Gornick
Anne George & the Royal College of Art library
Marion Wesel
Ed McDonald/Signa Design Group/USA
Clare Brass/Italy
Jane Dillon
Lynne Walker/RIBA
Michael Twyman/University of Reading
Gillian Naylor/Royal College of Art
Kathleen Schenck-Row/Designspace/USA
Lorraine Wild/CalArts/USA
Robin Kinross
Kate Symington
Sarah Reed
Lynne Wilson
Ellen Hackman & Ann O'Shea/USA
Michael Aminian
John Latimer Smith
Karen Mahony
Helen Macve
Linda Stubington
Ian Loveday
Lucy Bullivant
Thelma Agnew

Liz McQuiston (left) and colleague Julia King, taking a break.

# Katrin Adam *architecture*

**Biography**
Born 1938 in Munich, Germany.
Education: Cabinetmaking Guild
of Munich, Journeyman
Certificate, Cabinetmaking and
Carpentry, 1957; Beaux Arts
Academy, BA Interior
Architecture, Munich, 1964.
Design Experience: Junior
Designer with Nora Gad and
Aryle L Noy, Architects, Tel
Aviv, Israel, 1962; Designer with
Eero Saarinen & Associates
Architects (Roche, Dinkeloo &
Associates), New Haven,
Connecticut, USA, 1967–70;
Designer, worked with Pico
Union Neighbourhood Council,
Frank O Gehry and Associates,
Charles Kratka Associates, and
Kurt Meyer and Associates
Architects, in Los Angeles,
California, 1970–73; Co-founder
and Design Co-ordinator of the
Women's Development
Corporation, Providence, Rhode
Island, 1979–81; private practice
– architecture, planning and
development projects, 1973.
Projects for the Public Sector
include: residential projects –
Greenpoint Hospital
Intergenerational Housing
Project; 66 Avenue C and 606
East 11th Street (Urban
Homesteading Projects); for the
New York City Transit Authority
– Subway Station Rehabilitation;
Engineering Survey and Report;
institutional projects – Middle
Village Senior Center and
Services Now for Adult Persons
Center (with NYC Department
for the Aging). For the Private
Sector: programming and design
of Ralph J Bunche Day Care
Center, United Nations, NYC;
architectural, interior and
furniture design services for new
store and new office installations
in NYC; various private
residences. Work featured in
magazines and journals,
internationally. Grants and
Awards include: National
Endowment for the Arts, 1983;
American Planning Association
(competition), 1980; Community
Service and Economic
Development Administration,
Washington DC, 1979. Teaching
Experience: Women's School of
Planning and Architecture, 1978,
and the School of Architecture
and Environmental Studies, City
College, City University of New
York, 1976.

Katrin Adam runs an independent architectural practice in New York City. She is committed to non-elitist, participatory architecture . . . what she calls 'social architecture – really working with people to improve their environment'. Her practice, consequently, involves a precarious balancing of profit making commercial projects, and limited-income producing, socially oriented projects – which are the 'heart and soul' of her work.

She was born and educated in Munich, Germany. After her studies, she travelled to America and worked in design firms on both the East and West Coasts before eventually deciding to settle in New York City. She established her architectural office there in 1973 and in addition to maintaining a demanding practice, has been an active supporter of women in the profession. She was co-founder of the Women's School of Planning and Architecture, and was also co-founder and design co-ordinator (1979–81) for the Women's Development Corporation in Providence, Rhode Island. This is a non-profit organisation established to design and build user-responsive residential and commercial space with and for low income women and single parents. It also develops job opportunities and training for women in the field of housing development.

Her social commitment, as well as her work methods and interests, are best described by her recent public housing projects for underprivileged urban areas. These projects concentrate on exploring models that are responsive to the changing needs of various households – for example, single parents, working parents, the elderly, teenage mothers. They also involve future home users in the design and construction process by means of a series of participatory exercises which Katrin Adam developed.

On the commercial side, Katrin Adam's projects include architectural, interior and furniture design services for new office and new store installations in New York City: for example, the design of the New York Office of Pentagram, a leading international graphic design firm; and offices, wholesale showrooms and stores for large fashion companies.

How do the two worlds co-exist within her design practice? Not all that comfortably as she briefly explains the difficulty in balancing her desire to work on 'social architecture' and the necessity of maintaining a solvent financial position . . .

'My (social) projects are not self-supporting and I have to take on any job that comes into the office. Many are private sector, 'establishment' jobs which come to us via recommendations of former clients. It's not easy to focus on people who have money and one set of needs, and then to re-focus on people who have none and very different needs. Attempting to be accepted in both worlds is very trying . . .

'It is difficult for lower income people to understand why you do work for a corporation. It is equally difficult for a corporation to consider you suitable to handle their problems if you also do work for lower income families. You are typecast by both – you are either an establishment person and you do establishment work, or you are a grass roots person and work with the community/public sector. You must constantly be prepared to be questioned by both worlds.

'I find there is a constant battle between finding emotional satisfaction and feeling good about the way I use my architectural skills, and financial survival supported by a world of privilege that provides substantial design budgets but not enough personal meaning for me. The values of the two worlds are so different: for a corporation, a light fixture that costs seventy dollars is cheap; for the person on the Lower East Side this cost is overwhelming. I constantly have to juggle those different value systems, always trying to give my best to both – in terms of good design and a finished, quality product.'

Katrin Adam (in the middle) and friends

*Our intentions and concerns:*

*We want to create a structure which makes the skills of an architect available to those in most need.*

*We are committed to supporting women.*

*We want to promote and accommodate, in our design work and our lives, the idea of a more integrated personal work life.*

*We want to reinforce others in the pursuit of gaining control of their housing situation and their environment.*

*We are committed to the idea that architecture must serve people.*

*We want our designs to be such that they allow for social change.*

*We want to change the presently established roles and work process between architect, builder and client.*

Left: A statement written by Katrin Adam's architectural office, early 1980s.

**Architectural Quality in Urban Homesteading**
New York City, NY, 1983–.
Katrin Adam Associates, Architects

A programme which aims to demonstrate that well designed and affordable housing for low and moderate income people can be created by providing a tool which enables homesteaders to get involved in the design, development and construction of their future housing. (This is achieved via a series of participatory exercises developed by Katrin Adam.) The programme involves the gut rehabilitation of two abandoned buildings in NYC's Lower East Side: one will create dwellings for women and single parent families; the other is to house elderly and handicapped people and displaced families. (Continued next page)

Left: Architects and home-steaders discussing plans.

11

## Architectural Quality in Urban Homesteading

**The Exercises**
The participatory exercises created for the homesteaders by Katrin Adam are briefly described as follows:

**Exercise 1**
Initial qualitative evaluation of the homesteaders' existing housing, to assess subjective attributes and deficiencies such as natural light, view, noise etc.

**Exercise 2**
Listing types and sizes of the homesteaders' existing furniture, so that it may be accommodated in their new home.

**Exercise 3**
Reading architectural drawings; learning to understand the transcription from actual space to two-dimensional drawings.

**Exercise 4**
Drawing the building to be homesteaded; homesteaders and architects review and record the entire building.

**Exercise 5**
Locating the individual dwelling units within the building; to consider the needs of the elderly, etc.

**Exercise 6**
Developing an awareness of the spacial potential of the units; to discover significant needs, considered a luxury by the homesteaders, which in reality can be obtained.

**Exercise 7**
Establishing the ambience and material and finish selection.

**Exercise 8**
Seminars for exploration and discussion: Mechanical systems and cost efficiency, Cost estimating, General contracting, Financing, Management, etc. etc.

**Exercise 9**
Homesteaders design their own apartments, with the guidance of the architect.

**Exercise 10**
Evaluating carpentry skills; to determine what the homesteaders are capable of building, and to explore means to improve that capability.

Above: Homesteaders' buildings, 66 Avenue C (left) and 606 East 11th Street (right).

Below: Homesteader's fantasy collage of his/her ideal dwelling (from Exercise 6).

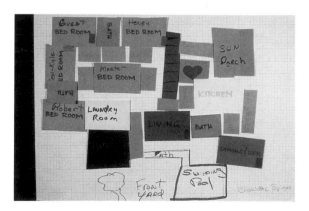

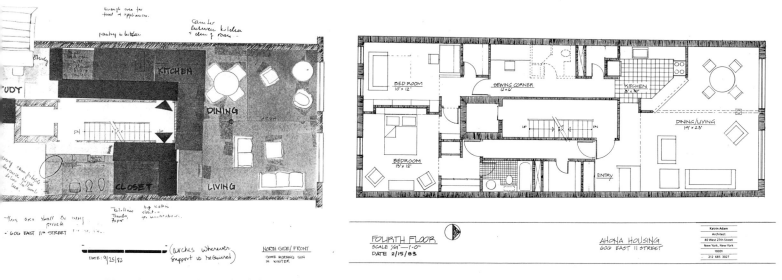

Above: Homesteader's collage of his/her apartment design (left), and architect's interpretation of homesteader's design (right).

Above: Homesteaders designing their own apartments (from Exercise 9), using the base perimeter plan, coloured paper representing different rooms, and paper cut-outs of furniture. See collage, top left of page.

Left: Woman reading architectural plans (Exercise 3).

Far left: Homesteaders heaving sheets of plywood onto the building at 66 Avenue C.

13

# Britain

# Hedda Beese *product design*

**Biography**
Born 1944 in Guhrau, Germany. Educated at: Padigogische Hochschule, Berlin, BA in Educational Sciences, 1968. Arrived in England, 1968; taught German and Art in local grammar schools, Ilford. Studied for second degree: Central School of Art and Design, London, BA in Industrial Design, 1976, and CSD Diploma with Distinction. Joined Moggridge Associates as Design Assistant 1976, appointed Designer 1978, appointed Associate and member of the Board of Design Developments 1979. Currently joint Managing Director, with John Stoddard, and is establishing a new product design division, Design Drei, in West Germany. Has lectured at: Central School of Art and Design, London; Royal College of Art, London; Newcastle Polytechnic; DZ Design Centre in Bilbao, conference on Industrial Design, 1987. Careers advisor to school leavers and to ILEA careers officers, London. Design Council Award for the STC Wide Area Radiopager, 1982. Exhibitions: 'Designers in Britain', Design Centre, London, 1980; '30 Ex-ILEA', Whitechapel Gallery, London, 1981; 'Designed in Britain, Made Abroad', Design Centre, London/Glasgow, 1981; ITT Europe Telephone selected for the Study Collection, Museum of Modern Art, New York, 1985; BP Solar Lantern, Innovation Centre, London, 1987; .'Design It Again', Design Centre, London/Glasgow, 1987. Elected member of the Panel A Product Design committee of the Chartered Society of Designers, 1978; appointed judge for 1981 Design Council Awards for Consumer and Contract Goods; appointed judge for the Royal Society of Arts Design Bursaries Competition, Small Electrical Goods, 1982; appointed judge for the Design Council's School Design Prize, 1983. Member of the Chartered Society of Designers; Fellow of the Royal Society of Arts, London, 1983.

Product design is German-born Hedda Beese's second career. She received her first degree in Education in Germany, and moved to London in 1968. She then taught German and Art at secondary level in London schools for about five years before eventually deciding to pursue a degree course in industrial design.

Roughly ten years on from gaining her second degree, she is now Joint Managing Director (with John Stoddard) of Moggridge Associates, a leading British product design consultancy with a reputation for innovative product development.

Hedda Beese is also on the Company Board of Directors of Design Developments Ltd, which includes the three divisions of Moggridge Associates (product design), IDM (modelmaking) and ID Two (product design) in San Francisco – and she is currently establishing a new product design division, Design Drei, in West Germany. Here she writes a few notes on what excites her about designing:

'I think I was lucky that design crossed my path in many guises over a long period of time before I recognised it. A strong feeling of commitment and sense of purpose took hold when I decided at 29 to study for my second degree, and there was no end of satisfaction and pleasure when it all fell into place.

Being a designer allows me some very individual approaches and responses to people. Next to language and physical expression, I find the objects people choose to have, or not to have, around them to be the most powerful indicator of their values and culture, and the most fascinating one to observe.

Little can compete with the excitement of arriving in a new country with all your senses alert, absorbing millions of individual impressions which gradually contribute to a more complex and forever changing picture of a new place. Visiting a client for your first briefing meeting has quite similar qualities. You are confronted with an intricate sub-culture, there to be read and interpreted quickly and correctly. You have

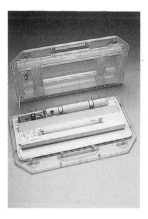

Above: Open view of the BP Solar Lantern.

BP Solar Lantern, designed 1985.
'The SL 48 Solar Lantern is a product precedent made possible by the use of new technology. Converting sunlight into electricity through silicon cells, the batteries are charged during sunshine hours to provide the equivalent of 4 hours of 40 watt light. It is designed for carrying, hanging or standing. High durability, extreme robustness and virtually zero maintenance were of prime importance. Moulded in polycarbonate, the lantern had to be environmentally sealed and able to perform under extreme temperatures.'

Moggridge Associates, Watering Can, designed 1987. 'A visual exercise in style for a product type deserving more attention to design than it generally receives.'

to respond to it in a manner that turns your outsider role to advantage, and prepares the way for a receptive climate from there on.

I never fail to be thrilled, knowing that I am in a client meeting because people have confidence in my ability to contribute aspects to the process of developing new products that could not come from within their company alone. Having an outsider's frame of reference, and a looser, less burdened approach to the problem in hand, certainly helps to create ideas of a sometimes unexpected nature.

I see my role very much as the ambassador for the end user, as well as the moderator between the conflicting requirements and partisan interests within the client companies: a very absorbing task.

And then there is the design process itself: the product planning and marketing approach, the anticipation of future events and people's responses to this not yet existing object; the optimisation of simple or complex usage aspects, by observation and involvement of real people – not just designers' assumptions about them; the solutions to the functional and technical aspects of manufacture; and tying all these elements together and giving them a form of expression – with aesthetic qualities which will give the product a unique character, loaded with a multitude of visual clues that people will respond to. The form you finally devise will provide access to the product – intellectual and emotional – or block it, if there is no convincing underlying concept.

What I like about designing is . . . the touch of the unexpected, the cunningly simple, the not obvious and yet not contrived, the lastingly stimulating, delightful, and sensuous, the interplay of opposites, the resolved tensions, the absence of dogma and unshakable rules, the sophisticated attention to detail, the finely tuned balance of all elements contributing to the process, the highest quality of thought – ultimately reflecting care about people rather than objects.'

Hedda Beese

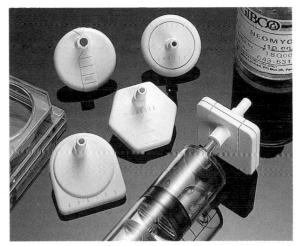

STC, Wide Area Radiopager, designed 1978. 'Innovative electronic design provided the challenge and opportunity to design the smallest radiopager of its time. The overall aim was to arrive at a form that would be pleasant to handle and comfortable when worn. The controls are recessed to avoid accidental operation yet placed in easily accessible positions. The complete assembly snaps together without any screws or additional fittings. The pager won a British Design Council Award for Advanced Technology and Excellent Industrial Design in 1982.'

Anotec Separations, Disposable Syringe Filter Housings, designed 1986. 'A new inorganic filter material with a uniquely fine and uniform pore size had been developed. The first product application was found in disposable syringe filters for laboratory use. Five proposals were developed to appearance model stage and an off-centre inlet and outlet was recommended to enable easy viewing of the sample while filtering from the syringe. The hexagonal external shape was eventually selected because of its distinctive appearance.'

# Italy

# Cini Boeri *architecture and design*

**Biography**
Born 1924 in Milan, Italy.
Educated at: the 'Politecnico' of
Milan, graduated in 1950.
Collaborated with Marco Zanuso,
and then began independent
professional activities in 1963,
applying herself to civil and
interior architecture and
industrial design. Selected
projects and architectural works:
show-rooms for Knoll
International, Los Angeles,
Stuttgart, Paris, Milan, Foligno
and New York, 1975–85; project
for a series of prefabricated
single-family houses, for Misawa
Company of Tokyo, 1983; offices
for Shearson Lehman, Milan,
1987; and various banks, offices,
galleries, museums, and villas.
Project and reconversion of many
apartments in Italy, France,
Japan, Switzerland and the USA.
In the field of industrial design,
she has worked for leading firms
such as Arflex/Milan, Artemide/
Milan, Rosenthal/Germany,
Knoll International/USA and
Europe, and others. She has
participated in many exhibitions,
including: '16 donne designers
Italiane', Tokyo, 1985; and
'Progetto Domestico', Milan
Triennale, 1986 (with a project
regarding 'human dimensions').
Visiting Professor in the Faculty
of Architecture, Polytecnic,
Milan, 1980. Jury Member for
numerous international
competitions: 'Deltas',
Barcelona, 1976; International
Chair Design Competition, San
Diego, 1976; 'A Decade of
Excellence in Interior
Architecture', San Francisco,
1979; Stigler Otis Competition,
Milan, 1982; 'Progressive
Architecture – Third Annual
International Furniture
Competition', New York, 1984;
Compasso d'Oro Jury, Milan,
1984. Awards include: Mention,
Compasso d'Oro, 1970;
Compasso d'Oro, 1979; Gold
Medal, BIO 10, Ljubljana, 1984;
and award 'DESIGN 85', Design
Center Stuttgart, 1984. She
published the book *The Human
Dimensions of the House*, with the
editor F Angeli in 1980, and has
lectured in universities & colleges
in Spain, Brazil, & the USA.

The name Cini Boeri has come to represent the best
in classical Italian design. For the last 20-odd years,
Cini Boeri has been a leading figure in Italian design
and her work is admired the world over for its
integrity, seriousness and diversity (her studio
tackles everything from light fittings to buildings).

A statement concerning work and design attitudes
follows from Cini Boeri herself:

'My work as a designer is certainly better known than
that as an architect, but in Italy the culture of design
is inextricably linked with that of architecture and
consequently I have simultaneously carried on both
activities. The anthropocentric character which the
disciplines of architecture and design have in
common is what I have chosen as the theme of my
work. I have worked principally on dwelling spaces,
that is to say the residential interior: on the human
dimension of architecture, on the floorplan of the
house rather than its image. And I have researched
the object as a necessary accessory to the life of man:
man in relation with the social and the private sphere.
Architecture is, par excellence, something human,
and for the man who lives and inhabits architecture it
should offer the essential: warmth, the pleasures of
feeling secure, simplicity and the joy of the natural
elements. It should not be an image of anxiety, a
symbol of futility, an expression of grandeur.

I have thus tried to work in this framework. The
few built homes, the many new and renovated
apartments I have designed, are all evidence of the
priority that I have always given to the vital demands
of the dwelling. I have always studied the
distribution of interior space by attempting to
provide the individual with privacy, and at the same
time offering the possibility and choice of interaction
with others in common spaces. I have also conducted
research into alternative dwellings for groups other
than the traditional family, and I have done much
work in the field of industrial design. Here I
experimented with and proposed a broader
functional dynamic for the object, and for a way of
life which is more in harmony with real necessities,
and less tied to tradition.

The values which I considered to be primary in the
design of these objects have been flexibility of use,

Cini Boeri

the concentration of a greater number of functions in
smaller dimensions, the negation of apparent
symbolism, and the tendency to offer an easier
lifestyle, less conventional and more personal.

From time to time I tried to propose low-cost
objects in the hope that industry would market the
product to be available to everyone, but the results
have turned out differently. Design means the
project, and, in this sense, the planning: a tension
towards the future, anticipation of what is already
possible but not yet real. The world is the field in
which this design creativity must be expressed and it
cannot exclude a reflection on human life.'

Lampada Chiara, prod.
Venini, 1984.
Lamp in blown glass,
designed in three different
versions: floor lamp, table
lamp and suspended lamp.

17

Left: Tavolo Malibù, prod.
Arflex, 1983.
'A series of rotating tables
using a pivot inserted in a
base containing drawers with
removable trays. The pivot,
with a rotation of 360°,
allows the top to be placed
directly above the base, out
of use, or outwards, allowing
dining room for six people.'

Below: 'Voyeur', prod.
Fiam, 1987.
Screen in curved, sand-
blasted glass with base and
frame in burnished steel.

Below: The Malibu table

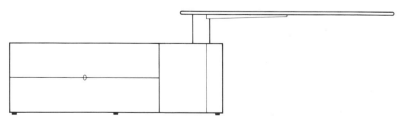

Left: Holiday house in
Sardinia, arch. Cini Boeri,
1967.

Left: Reconversion of the
Banca Popolare Di Verona,
Verona, 1980.

# Sheila Levrant de Bretteville *graphic design*

**Biography**
Born 1940 in Brooklyn, New York, USA. Educated at: Columbia University, Barnard College, A.B. degree in art history, New York, 1962; Yale University, USA, School of Art and Architecture, MFA in graphics, 1964. Consulation and design includes: Olivetti in Milan, Britain and Scandinavia, 1967–69; Universal Studios, film title proposal for 'The Big Fix', California, 1978; and redesign of the *Los Angeles Times*, California, 1979–80. Publication design includes: *Chrysalis*, a quarterly magazine of women's culture, Design Director and Member of Editorial Board, 1977–79; two books documenting Judy Chicago's 'The Dinner Party', Doubleday/Anchor Press, 1978–79; and logo and format for American Cinematographer, 1983; and many others. Has designed logos, letterheads, posters, signage, catalogs and brochures for various clients. Co-founder and President of 'The Woman's Building', a public center for women's culture, Los Angeles, 1973–81; organized the first 'National Women in Design' conference, and the first 'Women in the Printing Arts' exhibition, the Woman's Building, 1974. Director of the Women's Graphic Center since 1971 – founded the alternative educational program and laboratory facility. Initiated the Graphic Laboratory and the first Women's Design Program at the California Institute of the Arts, School of Design, 1970–72. Chair of Communication Design and Illustration, Otis Art Institute of Parsons School of Design, Los Angeles, 1981–. Has delivered many guest lectures, conducted workshops, and served as guest juror on design panels, nationwide. Awards include: 'Outstanding Educator of the Year', Who's Who in American Art, Who's Who in American Women; Grand Awards of Excellence, Society of Publication Designers, 1971; New York Type Directors Club, 1971, 1972. Her work has been exhibited throughout the USA.

The distinctive quality of Sheila de Bretteville's graphic design work has much to do with the strong sense of humanity that motivates it. And her projects are extremely varied, ranging from high-profile design briefs, such as the 1980 redesign of the *Los Angeles Times* (and Times New Roman Bold) – to jobs of a more personal nature, such as the creation of an identity (and much needed exposure) for a shop owner starting up a small business . . .

de Bretteville holds a degree in art history from Barnard College, Columbia University and a Masters degree in graphic design from Yale University's School of Art. In 1971, she created the first women's design programme at California Institute of the Arts, and in 1973 founded the Women's Graphic Centre at the Woman's Building, a public centre for women's culture in Los Angeles. Since 1982 she has chaired the Department of Communication Design and Illustration at Otis Art Institute of Parsons School of Design in Los Angeles; and she also runs her own design studio in LA.

Sheila de Bretteville writes about motivation and meaning in her work, both past and present . . .

'You ask: What is it about working in the field of graphic design that I most want to talk about at this point?

I answer: I see that I continually need to find or give meaning to the activity of graphic design. It is still wonderful, still fraught with contradictions. I keep wanting more from the activity, pushing at its edges, critiquing the center.

I am in the business of giving meaning to my work, understanding why and for whom I do what I do. This inquiry informs the graphic work I do for clients as well as that which I initiate myself; it shapes the course of the program I chair at Otis/Parsons, sparks the class I am currently teaching on cultural diversity as well as the boxes I have begun to make for myself to learn about myself.

While still a student of art history in college, I decided I didn't want to become a professor or work in a museum. There didn't seem to be enough contact with people – just regular, everyday people – in that work. So I developed myself as a graphic designer, thinking that graphics would combine this thirst for contact with the street and people, with my love of what is thoughtfully made, clearly crafted and communicated.

Like many designers, I have a need to make things that "ring true", that have a close fit between what I intend to communicate and what the viewer/reader sees being said. I like my working process to surprise and teach me, leading me to solutions I could not have totally predicted at the onset. And I need to feel that the work contributes something that there isn't enough of in the world already. Not only do I want to learn through my graphic work and enhance my life, but I want the viewer/user to learn and have his or her life enhanced too!

Oh, that does get to be a heavy load for graphic work to carry – this service activity created to package and sell ideas and products. I do slide sometimes into simply doing a caring and careful, traditional job – a catalog for an artist, newspaper spreads of athletic accomplishments, an announcement for the opening of a library – only mildly expressing those places where my sensibility and values overlap with theirs. But mostly, and certainly this is the work with which I have the deeper connection, I try to position myself to be able to use my graphic skills for subjects and clients with whom I have a vital connection – including myself!

Early in my career I began to augment my work for museums, presses – traditional corporate, cultural and commercial clients – with work for neighborhoods, graphics about women in society, and teaching. I found that my teaching and my graphic work shared a method: fostering dialog and reciprocity.

Perhaps a clear listing of some of the methods I see inviting dialog by evoking the viewers' thoughtful response would be of use:

*1. The inclusion of several perspectives on the same subject* indicates that the viewpoint of the viewer is likewise welcome. The grid appears to be the simplest method for organising messages so that they can be seen as equal in importance by being received in any order chosen by the viewer. A more hierarchical organization would lead the viewer through the content provided – a more usual expression of diverse views.

*2. Asking a question without providing an answer* requires a response from the viewer so that the conversation can continue. As the narrator or speaker is not there to participate further in the conversation, information about where the dialog could continue would be useful.

*3. Providing evocative but not explicit views of the subject matter* involves the receiver in a quest for meaning. Images predominate in the method and many possible readings coexist. The designer has to be willing to have the viewer create meanings that he or she could not have foretold.

I continue to be exhilarated by a vision of graphic design functioning in much the same way Paulo Friere describes his class in *Education for Critical Consciousness*, as "a meetingplace where knowledge is sought, not where it is transmitted". This notion has led me to various kinds of graphic formats where there wasn't one answer but multiple voices. Information is given but it is not a closed declaration and a response is requested, directly or indirectly. The principle behind this exchange and encouragement of ideas is the initiation of dialog, connection and community.'

Sheila Levrant de Bretteville

Right: 'Wilder Place', ad in *L.A. Style*, December 1986.

Below right: 'Wilder Place' storefront, Fall 1986.

'This project is most expressive of my need to respond when someone else is desperate. I feel resistant to using graphics to sell superfluous merchandise, yet I enjoyed helping Jo make her small shop visible. It was the first business she had on her own – she was reaching out, making herself and what she enjoyed doing public and known. There is an exuberance and spirit in her eclectic shop that I tried to give a voice – very quickly and inexpensively as she was unpacking her boxes without anything up in the street or in the mails to announce her presence.'

design collection

wrench bowl $265

also

jewelry
books
furniture
...

WILDER
PLACE

7975½ Melrose Avenue
Los Angeles, CA 90046

213 655-9072

Friday & Saturday 10-10
Monday – Thursday 10-6

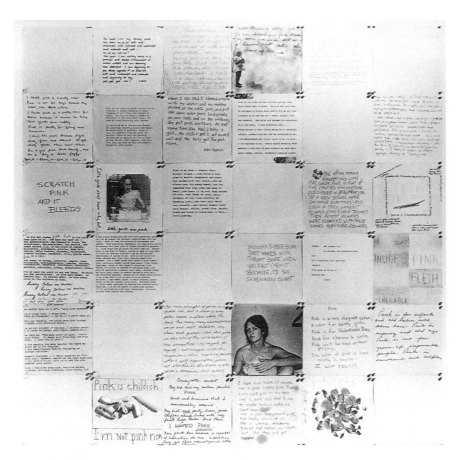

Left: 'Pink', a one of a kind created in response to a request from the AIGA, then made into a poster and put up in the streets of L.A. (above), 1974.

'One hundred artists and designers were asked by the American Institute of Graphic Arts to "say something about color" on a thirty-inch square format for an exhibition at the Whitney Museum. I divided the space given me into a grid of 36 equal squares and asked women of varying backgrounds and ages to contribute their views on the meaning of the color pink, which they wrote or depicted in most of the squares. I reproduced the result as posters and personally put them up in the streets of Los Angeles, exposing the viewers to multiple meanings and encouraging them to think what pink meant to them and their vision of women. People wrote their views on the clear pink squares left open for that purpose and discussed among themselves the obvious subject of the poster: women and the attributes associated with them and with the colour pink.'

Left: Grand Central Market construction barricade, 1987.

'Putting the Pink poster up in the streets led me to thinking about who the client really is for graphic work, and to add to the paying client the people who would see the work. More than ten years after "Pink", I was asked to design a construction barricade for a market about to be renovated, across the street from an old people's home in an ethnically diverse neighborhood. The barricade has been up for a year unmarked by graffiti and the people whose memories – written out in their own languages and with credit for their words – are tucked among the fruits and vegetables tell me that not only are their families proud but they feel like honored members of the community. This is a project that seems to give back to everyone involved; the developer who was the paying client, the students who interviewed the old people in their own languages, the people whose feelings were made public, and me, the designer who gets a personal pleasure from the street and creating ways in which people who are not generally heard from, speak and are heard.'

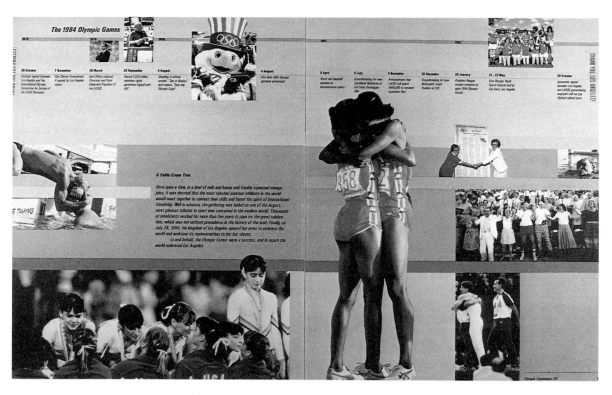

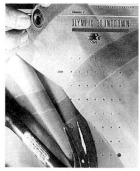

Above and left: Cover and spreads from Olympic inserts in the Sunday magazine section of the *Los Angeles Times*, 1984.

'Before the Olympics I designed a monthly insert into the Sunday section of the *Los Angeles Times*. Most of the spreads were like the cover image of the Olympic banners being prepared – lightly descriptive, full color images and "soft news". But for the final issue, while everyone was too busy at the Olympics to provide copy or images, I created a time line out of the ubiquitous colored rules – giving more specific meaning(s) to the modernist abstraction. I take particular pleasure in being able to add to the spread about the moment of singular success, a spread of the pleasure in the success of others, using all the images I could find of the congratulatory hands, hugs and kisses.'

# USA   **Denise Scott Brown** *architecture and urbanism*

**Biography**
Born 1931 in Nkana, Zambia.
Educated at: Architectural
Association, London, 1952–55,
AA Diploma and Certificate in
Tropical Architecture, 1956.
Emigrated to USA 1958.
University of Pennsylvania, M.
City Planning, 1960, and M.
Arch, 1965. Has worked with
Venturi and Rauch since 1967;
Architect, Planner – then
Partner. Teaching experience
includes; Assistant Professor,
University of Pennsylvania,
School of Fine Arts, 1960–65,
Visiting Professor, 1982 and
1983; Associate Professor,
University of California, Los
Angeles, School of Architecture
and Urban Planning, (initiated
Urban Design Program), 1965–
68; Visiting Professor in Urban
Design, Yale University,
Department of Architecture,
1967–70; and several hundred
lectures, conferences, jury and
selection panels, in Europe,
America and Africa, 1960–.
Member of: Advisory
Committee, Temple University,
Department of Agriculture,
1980–; Philadelphia Jewish
Children's Folkshul, Curriculum
and Adult Education
Committees, 1980–; Advisor to
the National Trust for Historic
Preservation, National Main
Street Center, 1981–; member of
the Board of Directors, Central
Philadelphia Development
Corporation, 1985–; and others.
Has received honorary degrees
from several institutions. Urban
Design and Planning Project
Awards, include: National
Endowment for the Arts, Design
Arts Program, Recognition
Awards – 'The Strand Planning
Study', 'Signs of Life – Symbols
in the American City Exhibition'
(film), 'City Edges – Schuykill
River Corridor Study', 1980;
Progressive Architecture Annual
Awards, Urban Design and
Planning, citation – 'Jim Thorpe
Planning Study', 1980,
'Princeton Urban Design Study',
1981, 'Washington Avenue,
Miami Beach', 1982; HUD
National Awards for Urban
Environmental Design, Urban
Design Administration, Honor
Award for 'Old City Study and
Facade Easement Program',
1980. Has written extensively on
architecture and planning.

Denise Scott Brown is a partner in the leading American architectural design firm of Venturi, Rauch and Scott Brown. She describes her current work and broad interests in the statement that follows:

'During 1987, I worked on two projects in parallel, the one a plan for downtown Memphis, Tennessee, the other the design of the extension to the National Gallery in London.

For Memphis, I was the principal in charge of an interdisciplinary team of eight consultants: economists, transportation engineers, architects, landscape architects, planners, urban designers, preservationists, cultural planners, and there was a special consultant hired to represent the interests of Memphis's black community. The demand on me was to span all these topics, and in so doing, guide the team in producing a plan that was truly interdisciplinary, not merely multidisciplinary. I was to ensure that, out of the city's flavorful culture and history, unique potential, and hard reality, a socially responsible beauty would emerge.

In the design of the National Gallery, where I was a collaborator on the project team, the challenge was in some ways the same: to bring out of *this* reality a container for paintings that are among the most precious treasures in the world, and to produce a good architectural neighbor in the untidy but evocative surroundings of Trafalgar Square.

These projects have in common that they are exciting intellectually and aesthetically; they must draw a, perhaps; agonized beauty from their reality; they call for social and moral responsibility; and they cover broad spans of concern. In Memphis, I must deal with the design of paving patterns and of regions, understand the principles of traffic forecasting, discuss funding mechanisms, learn the history of W C Handy and Elvis Presley, and know the meaning of the Reverend Martin Luther King's choice of hotels.

In London, I must advise on pedestrian flow in and around the Gallery; but I must also cogitate with others on the nature of wall surfaces that will do justice to precious paintings, and on how to bring four million people a year past delicately-scaled canvases, without compromising their safety or destroying their ability to touch the individual. It has been a challenge too, to use my English experience to help interpret London and the requirements of our English client to my colleagues.

In each project the time span is from the most immediate to the distant past and future. The link we are reforging between Memphis and the Mississippi can last a thousand years. The National Gallery's early Renaissance paintings are part way through their first millennium; the building, with luck, should last another.

My good friend, the late Paul Davidoff, once said that architects who believe they can design everything from a teaspoon to a region have delusions of grandeur, and I have always agreed with him. It is therefore puzzling to see our practice span from the design of a teapot to the design of Westway. What intrigues is the mixture. To meet, responsibly, the requirements of our variety of concerns, we must understand that a move from one scale to another, or from one discipline to another, involves a change of hats – you become a different person. We must know, as well, what we can't do; when we must find help. I am not a transportation planner but I know how to work with one. I can describe the social or urban design implications of the transportation plan (which the transportation planner may not know) and understand what I can legitimately ask of urban transportation facilities and their planner.

I am an architect and planner, not an architect-planner. My span of interests proceeds beyond these fields, toward the decorative arts in one direction and social planning and the social sciences in the other. In addition, I like to write and teach and am involved deeply in the management of my firm, in marketing and in helping to maintain an administrative structure that will keep us as creative as we can be.

My work spans several axes: between the academic and the professional, theory and practice; between small and large; between administration and execution; and across three continents and a range of disciplines. My window on the world is architecture, the focus of my greatest personal responsibility is on urban design – or perhaps it is on the connections between things.'

**Washington Avenue Revitalization Plan**

Planning study for the preservation of a shopping street in Miami Beach, Florida, 1978.
In collaboration with David Jay Feinberg and Richard Rose, Architects.
In charge:
Denise Scott Brown.
Project architect: Mary Yee with David Brisbin, Francis Hundt, Steven Izenour, James Allen Schmidt, Frederic Schwartz, James H Timberlake.

'This project, undertaken in association with David Jay Feinberg, Architect, involved the study of the economic, social and transportation functions, the design of street and landscape improvements, and the setting out of design guidelines for the commercial spine that runs through the center of Miami Beach's Art Deco District and serves as its main street.

This corridor connects the City's two largest-scale redevelopment projects. Its unique features are the demographic mix of its major user groups – senior citizen and ethnic populations – its Art Deco architecture and its tropical landscape. 'An incremental approach involving small scale improvements was suggested. The work included detailed surveying of the physical and commercial aspects of Washington Avenue, a general analysis of its role in the city's and region's economy, recommendations for land use, an outline of alternative development strategies for the future, design of public sector improvements, design guidelines for future private and public improvements, recommendations for the implementation of aesthetic guidelines, a capital program, and an action plan for the funding and staging of capital improvements.'

Below: Denise Scott Brown

Above: View south on Washington Avenue at 15th Street, Miami Beach, Florida (drawing: Frederic Schwartz).

Above: Recommendations for shop fronts, Washington Avenue, Miami Beach, Florida (drawing: John Colesberry and Frederic Schwartz).

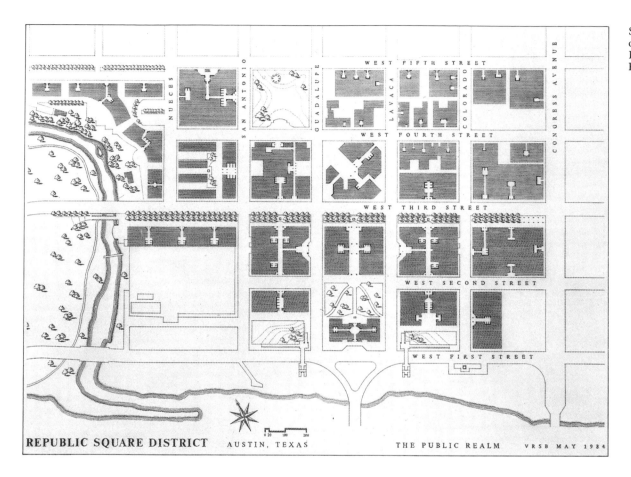

REPUBLIC SQUARE DISTRICT    AUSTIN, TEXAS    THE PUBLIC REALM    VRSB MAY 1984

Site Plan for the public realm of the Republic Square District (drawing: Miles Ritter).

## Republic Square District Master Plan

Renewal plan for a downtown district in Austin, Texas, 1983.
In collaboration with Halcyon Ltd, Economists.
In charge:
Denise Scott Brown.
Project manager:
Vincent Hauser
with Gabrielle London, Miles Ritter, David Schaaf, Robert Venturi.

'The Republic Square District, in Austin, Texas, is a former warehouse district that lies directly in the path of future downtown growth and contains a site that was proposed for Austin's future City Hall complex. The plan envisioned residential, governmental, office, hotel and community uses which meet at mixed-use "swing" blocks and are seamed together at street level through retail uses and a structure of civic spaces, designed with the Austin climate, landscape and ethos in mind. We recommended planting a tree-lined avenue beside West Third Street to serve as the main axis of the new business district, and suggested naming the street "The Rambla", alluding to Barcelona's famous avenue "Las Ramblas".'

## The Presentation

'The Rambla is set to one side of Third Street in order to maintain a pedestrian flow beside retail uses. Because Third Street traffic is one way, there is no reason to place the walkway on a median strip. In addition, we have tried to keep The Rambla narrow in order to maintain the linkage between retail fronts on either side of Third Street. The Rambla trees should be of moderate height and broad canopy; we prefer the traditional shape of the live oak, but if live oaks would not do well in such a location, perhaps another Texas shade tree could be found.
'A prime function of The Rambla will be lunch hour strolling, brown-bagging, sitting, and watching. Even in winter, it should be possible, at mid-day, to sit out on a bench, bundled up warmly, and enjoy the break from heated office space. During the summer, The Rambla, at its hottest, can still provide a respite from the onslaughts of air conditioning. Therefore, between trees there are benches, paired back to back to face into and away from The Rambla. Sidewalk cafes

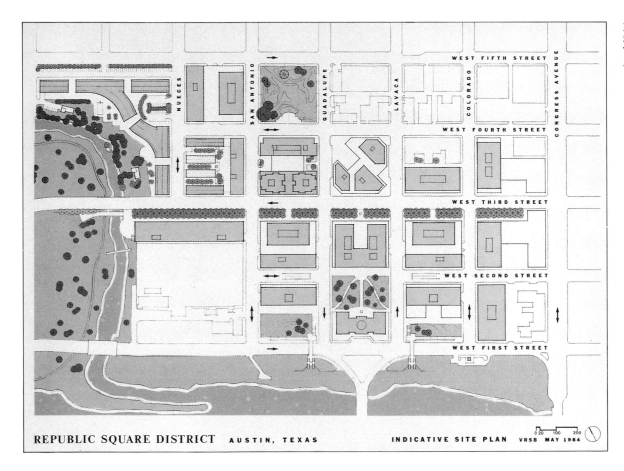

Indicative site plan, Republic Square District, Austin, Texas (drawing: Robert Marker).

REPUBLIC SQUARE DISTRICT    AUSTIN, TEXAS        INDICATIVE SITE PLAN    VRSB MAY 1984

can serve from abutting stores onto The Rambla. Entry points to buildings can be marked by kiosks, statues or fountains. Second and third floor office and retail uses will have a pleasant view of foliage. We would like to see The Rambla installed all at once and early, to be in position before the first office building on the south side opens.

'The Rambla is a simple facility that will be outstanding through its location, length and use. Although simple in concept, it ties the new development to the Austin love of outdoors and to the traditional landscape, in a highly urbanistic way; and it will provide a framework that can evoke many ideas for its use. Its evocative quality will contribute to the vitality of the District.'

Right: Sketch of 'The Rambla' (drawing: David Schaaf).

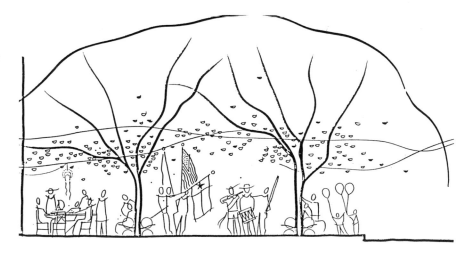

27

# USA     Frances Butler *design history, research and practice*

**Biography**
Born 1940 in St Louis, Missouri, USA. Educated at: University of California, Berkeley, BA History, 1961; Stanford University, MA History, 1963; University of California, MA Design, 1966; University of California, Berkeley, Department of Architecture, PhD advanced to candidacy, September 1987. Acting Instructor, University of California, Berkeley, Design Department, 1968–70, and Professor, Department of Environmental Design, 1970–. Proprietor of: Goodstuffs Handprinted Fabrics, Emeryville, California, 1973–79, Oakland, 1987; Poltroon Press, Berkeley, and Oakland, California, 1975–. Awards: National Endowment for the Arts Craftsmans Grant, 1973; National Endowment for the Arts Small Press Grant, 1977; National Endowment for the Arts Services to the Field, 1979; National Endowment for the Arts Artist Book, 1980. Artist in Residence at: Visual Studies Workshop, Rochester, New York, 1984; San Francisco Center for Interdisciplinary and Experimental Studies, 1985; School of the Art Institute of Chicago, 1986–87; and Banff Center for the Arts, Alberta, Canada, August 1987. Publications: selected books by Poltroon Press – *Confracti Mundi Rudera*, 1975; *New Dryads (are ready for your call)*, 1980; Occult Psychogenic Misfeasance, 1980; *Gon-Bop Deluxe*, 1983; *Career Options: A Catalog of Screens*, 1985; *Light and Heavy Light: Contemporary Shadow Use in the Visual Arts*, 1985; *Temporary Territories*, 1987; *Diaper Rash*, 1987; selected articles – 'The Persistance of Memory: Graphic Designers in the 1950s', *Arts and Architecture Magazine*, Vol 2 No 2, 1983, pp26–30; 'The Lesson of Things: The Fabric of Society & The Intentional Fallacy', *Design Book Review*, Vol 2 No 4, 1984, pp76–83; 'Two Poetry Gardens: Giving a Voice to the Genius Loci', *Places*, MIT Press, Vol 1 No 4, 1985, pp68–75; and many others. Her work has been exhibited in many galleries and museums both nationally and internationally.

Frances Butler is currently Professor of Environmental Design at University of California, Davis. Her 'design life', as she puts it, has been broad-based, full of experimentation, and highly prolific – whether speaking of the many fabric designs she has created for her company Goodstuffs, or the illustrated books she has produced through the Poltroon Press (a private press she founded in 1975 with Alastair Johnston). In her graphic work particularly she has exercised the relationship between language and image in a multitude of ways; the viewer is called upon to participate (mentally) and must connect isolated ideas into whole statements, pool associations from personal past and present, or grapple with visual metaphor and symbolism.

In all the areas of design in which she has worked her main interest has been to 'emphasize the perception of human activity'. In graphic design, she has concentrated on developing a visual language based on observation of human activity. This she describes as a pluralistic approach concerned with real human qualities, responses and feelings, as opposed to use of a graphic language based on fantasy stereotypes 'with rigidly stylized notions of gender and societal roles'.

Her broad activities are described, and a few heartfelt concerns laid on the line, in excerpts from the letter she wrote concerning her contribution to this book:

'I have an extremely varied past, and present, in design, having moved from being a fabric designer with my own company (selling fabric wall-hangings worldwide), to the ownership of a private press, publishing lavish books on poetry, typography, and book design (selling books worldwide), to my present dual concerns: writing on design, and making, and writing about, gardens, both sophisticated poetry gardens and ethnic and naive gardens. I am finishing a PhD in the History of Architecture program at the University of California, Berkeley, and am writing my dissertation on emigrant gardens as cognitive tools.

'I understand that the usual fate of someone like myself is not to be taken seriously because I have not stuck to one aspect of the traditional design field. However, I believe that only by joining understanding of what creative work entails with the critical and analytical approaches typical of theoretical writers can valid writing about design be produced, and I feel that my preparation for design writing is not only appropriate, but the best kind possible. I think I fit your category of design historian or researcher, although I continue to work on different kinds of projects. I am now writing a book on type design and layout, and have almost completed a book on vernacular gardens. I am as well finishing a shadow garden for the University Hospital in Seattle, Washington, a public art project, and beginning a large mosaic mural (in the tradition of Diego Rivera) for a civic housing project in San Francisco . . .

'I believe strongly that my varied approach to creativity, involving critical thinking and writing and active design and production, is one that should be opened to more designers, and I propagandize for this approach everywhere I speak. And I think that it is because I am a female, and was told that maybe I wasn't good enough for the design "profession" that I looked at it critically, discovered that I was not interested in fitting into its narrow, traditional niches, and was motivated to make this wide-open world for myself.'

Spread from the book *Confracti Mundi Rudera*, 1975.

Above: Worried Man, fabric, 1979.

Above: Frances Butler

Right: Table of Contents; wood, lino;
30in x 8ft x 30in(ht), 1983.

Frances Butler's small private garden in Berkeley, California, called 'Light and Heavy Light' or the 'Shadow Garden'.

'After enlisting the professional aid of a landscape designer, a gardener and an architect to achieve a garden that would express my interest in overlapping layers of pattern, I finally redesigned my garden myself. It incorporates more elements reflecting changing time than most gardens, because it is now a shadow garden. Shadows of words and texts move over the ground plane during the day, their location or even their presence depending not only on the weather but on the season. The garden is dominated by trellises on which sleds of wire mesh were laid to carry varied texts in large wood or plastic letters, casting shadows onto the ground. 'Finally, a traditional shadow theater was established in one corner of the garden, complete with shadow puppets. Thus the garden provides for layers of overlapping pattern at any hour of the day or night.'

Above right: Shadow Garden, 'Later' (L8R), 1983.

Right: Shadow Garden, 'Homage to P. Zwart', 1985.

Overview of Shadow Garden, 1983–87.

# USA

# Jacqueline Casey *graphic design*

**Biography**
Born in Massachusetts, USA.
Educated at: Massachusetts
College of Art, Certificate in
Fashion Design and Illustration,
and Bachelor of Fine Arts.
Following graduation, worked in
fashion illustration, advertising,
interior decorating and trade
publication. Graphic designer at
MIT since 1955; currently
Director of Design Services at
MIT. Exhibitions at: MIT
Hayden Corridor Gallery, 1972,
1979, 1983, 1984; Chelsea School
of Art, London, 1978; MIT
Burton House Gallery, 1979;
London College of Printing,
1980; MIT Museum 1985; and
numerous group exhibitions.
Examples of her work are in the
permanent collections of: the
Museum of Modern Art, New
York; the Cooper-Hewitt
Museum, New York; the USIA
and the Library of Congress. Has
been guest lecturer at the
Massachusetts College of Art,
Yale University, Carnegie-
Mellon University, and Simmons
College. Has judged several
national exhibitions. Served as a
panel member reviewing
government graphics for the
Visual Communications Section
of the National Endowment for
the Arts in Washington. Her
work has been shown in
numerous books, magazines, and
annuals. She is a member of the
Alliance Graphique
Internationale.

The graphic design work of Jacqueline Casey, Director of Design Services at MIT, has been exhibited in colleges, galleries and museums throughout the world. She is a major name, and her work at MIT (particularly in poster design) is present in any significant review of American graphic design over the last 25 years. To graphic designers educated in America in the late 1960s and early 1970s (including the author of this book!) she is representative of the highly influential Swiss graphics movement of that time, and one of the great masters of The Grid – which she mentions here . . .

'My introduction to graphic design began in 1955 when I joined Muriel Cooper who was the art director in MIT's Office of Publications. Muriel was also a graduate of the Massachusetts College of Art. I really learned about graphic design from Muriel on the job. As a matter of fact two of the most influential people in my work happened to be women. The second was Therese Moll, a Swiss designer who worked in our office in 1958 and who introduced me to the Grid, which I have been using ever since.

My objective as a graphic designer is to create a product that makes sense to me and my client, and can be understood by a larger audience. Before I start to design, I research the subject so that the work will be representative of it. I collect information and sometimes visual material from clients, libraries, museums, laboratories, and so on. I also try to use colors and materials which relate to the subject; and the typeface must fit into the whole design. Sometimes the type is used in a large display fashion and becomes the visual image itself.

Most of my posters have been created for the MIT Committee on the Visual arts; they publicize exhibitions at the Gallery at MIT. They are posted flat all over MIT in advance of the upcoming exhibition, and are also folded and mailed to a very wide and sophisticated art community.

Intimate Architecture Exhibition Poster, 1982.

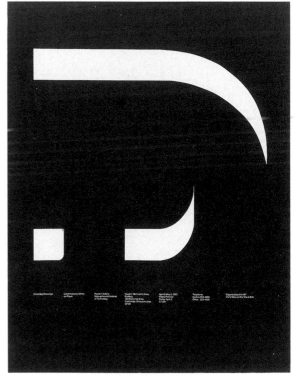

Great Big Drawings Exhibition Poster, 1982.

Most of the posters have black backgrounds for several reasons. Sometimes the Gallery is painted black or images are projected in the darkened room and the poster gives the viewer a small hint at what is to come. Because most of the bulletin boards at MIT are covered with small pieces of white and pastel paper, black shows up beautifully and is set off by the opposite color of the background. Finally, black or a dark color is a deterrent to graffiti. The posters in general have to carry a certain amount of information (often lengthy) but are meant to be viewed closely because the corridors are narrow and busy. My job is to stop anyone I can with an arresting or puzzling image, and entice the viewer to read the message in small type and above all to attend the exhibition.

The increase in the number of women and their contributions in the area of graphic design has been noteworthy, particularly in the last ten years. There were hardly any women art directors or graphic designers when I was starting out.'

Left: Jacqueline Casey

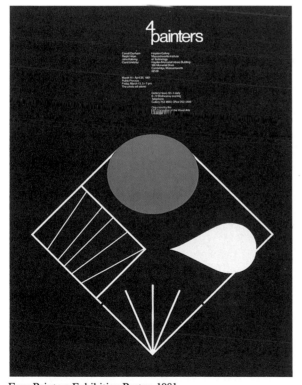

Four Painters Exhibition Poster, 1981.

Six Artists Exhibition Poster, 1970.

33

# USA   Muriel Cooper *graphic design and design research*

**Biography**
Professional experience: founded
Muriel Cooper Media Design,
1958, and is still its Principal;
first Design Director, MIT Office
of Publications (Design
Services), 1952–58; first Design
and Media Director, 1966–74 and
Special Projects Director, MIT
Press, 1966–78; co-founded New
Graphics Associates, 1983, and is
still its Principal. Associate
Professor of Visual Studies, MIT
Department of Architecture,
Media Laboratory, 1981–.
Previous academic appointments
at: Museum School of Fine Arts
(Boston); Simmons College;
Massachusetts College of Art;
Boston University; and the
University of Maryland. Has
presented numerous lectures,
symposia and workshops to a
wide variety of professional and
educational groups. Member of:
Massachusetts College of Art,
Board of Trustees (various
committees), 1981–; National
Endowment for the Arts, invited
panels, review committees, 1980–
84; Simmons College Advisory
Board, School of
Communication, 1982–;
American Institute of Graphic
Arts, Board member, frequent
service as Chair, Judge and Jury
member, 1960–80; Alliance
Graphique Internationale, 1982–;
Design Management Institute,
Board of Directors, 1984–; and
others. Selected Juried
Exhibitions (Graphic Design
Work), 1970–82: American
Association of University Press;
Printing Institute of America;
New York Type Director's Club;
New York Art Director's Club;
American Institute of Graphic
Arts. Awards include: Grand
Prix d'Arles, Design of Best
Photographic Book, 1974; Israel
Arts Book Biennale, Silver
Medal, 1982; Second AIGA
Design Leadership Award (to
MIT Design Services, MIT
Press, and the Visible Language
Workshop), 1982; Massachusetts
College of Art, Convocation
Presentation, 1983; and the
Distinguished Alumni Award,
Massachusetts College of Art,
1983. Of 500 books designed, art
directed and produced, 150 were
award books. Her work has
appeared in books on graphic
design, typography, and
computer graphics.

Muriel Cooper's outstanding contribution to design
at MIT was acknowledged when, in 1986, the
American Institute of Graphic Arts awarded its
second Design Leadership Award to the three MIT
graphics groups which she founded and led: Design
Services, The Media Department of the MIT Press
and, most recently, the Visible Language Workshop.
In the following statement she provides a quick scan
of background events and concerns, leading up to her
current role as Director of the VLW, a research
laboratory established 'to investigate the changes
implicit in the electronic revolution in relation to the
tradition, theory and practice of graphics, graphic
arts and visual communication'.

'For more than thirty years, my life and work have
been directed to visual communication expressed
through verbal and graphic means.

My concepts have always been synthesized with
media and technology and have included print,
photography, film, video, and three-dimensional
work. My professional activities have always been
interwoven with teaching and personal creative work.
I have had the good fortune to have had three distinct
"careers" at MIT: 1) the first designer and Art
Director of the Office of Publications (now Design
Services), 2) the first Media Director of the MIT
Press, and 3) the most challenging as the co-founder
and Director of the Visible Language Workshop.

As the challenges became more complex, my early
concerns evolved from surface relations and product,
to systems and problem-solving, to process and the
nature of communication. It became increasingly
apparent to me that attitudes and process were more
fundamental than individual solutions, and that there
were profound and disturbing contradictions in the
professional and educational environments which
were not being addressed from within.

I found the practice of graphic designers, and often
designers themselves, seriously constrained by the
limitations of print technology and by client directed
problems. In order to pursue more fundamental
issues, I deliberately chose to gradually phase out of
my professional practice as it was constituted.

During the years at the Office of Publications I was
absorbed with the exploration of the representation of
the differences and similarities of abstraction between
graphic representation and scientific and
technological concepts. In 1970, at the MIT Press, I

integrated the traditionally separate production and
design, and named it the Media Department to reflect
my growing concerns. Such a structure was intended
to enable research of new publishing forms: in-house
publishing and research into author-self publishing
issues; extended learning into and out of the
workplace; and the impact of growing electronic
communication issues on print patterns.

The goal, in my view, was to structure a group that
could respond creatively to change and where
research and practice could inform one another
iteratively. A great deal of innovative work was
accomplished and recognized but economic support
was not robust.

During those years, I joined the Architecture
Department as a part-time lecturer, working with
Ron MacNeil. Our work was seeded when the
Visible Language Workshop was established
officially with support from an interdisciplinary
group from Humanities, the MIT Press, the School
of Architecture and Planning, the Council for the
Arts, and the MIT Administration. In 1975, I was
appointed full time to the Architecture Department
and started building the VLW in earnest.

I wrote then that the Workshop was "a unique
laboratory in which the content, quality, and
technology of communication may be explored
and tested in a hands-on setting of educational,
professional, and research programs that provide
a learning triangle of experience, theory, and
application". The milieu has changed, but I believe
this continues to be valid.'

Muriel Cooper working in the Visible Language Workshop.

Muriel Cooper

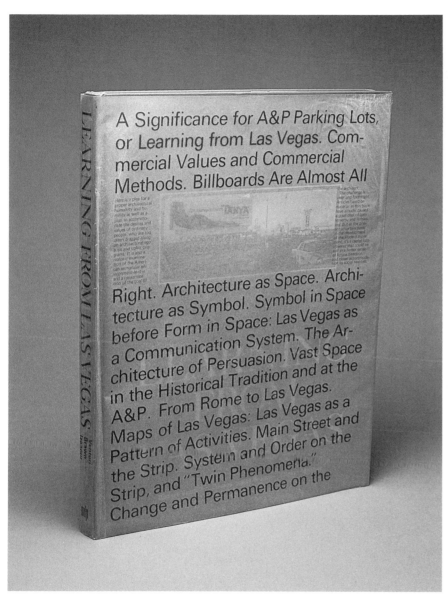

Book cover for *Learning from Las Vegas*.

Book cover and slipcase for *Bauhaus*.

# Britain

# Jane Dillon *furniture design*

**Biography**
Born 1943 in Manchester,
England. Education: NDD
Interior Design (Manchester)
1965; Royal College of Art,
London, MDes Furniture
Design, 1968. Design experience:
Knoll International UK, design
assistant, 1968–69; Consultant to
Olivetti (Milan) under Ettore
Sottsass – involved with office
furniture system 'Synthesi 45' as
colour consultant, and art
director for 'Synthesi 45'
catalogue, 1969–71; Office
planning consultant to Conran for
'Synthesi 45', 1971–72; 'Future of
the Office' research for Olivetti,
1971–72; Consultant to Casas
(Mobilplast, Barcelona) – office
and domestic seating in
collaboration with Charles Dillon,
ranges designed include 'Actis'
and 'Jobber'; Casas agents for
UK, Business Interiors, Bristol,
and for US, ICF, 1973 onwards;
Domestic lighting for Disform,
Barcelona, 1973; Consultant to
Habitat, ranges designed – 'Mesh'
shelving and 'Butterfly' lighting,
1977–78; Consultant to Wolff
Olins, including preparation for
the corporate and product
identity for Glynwedd, Faber
Castell, ENKA, 1978–79;
Consultant to Habitat/
Mothercare, ranges designed
include 'Quaker' and 'Strasse',
1982–85; experimental furniture
designs, one-off commissions;
small batch production runs for
architects (with Peter Wheeler
and Floris van den Broecke).
Visiting tutor: Royal College of
Art, 1968–; Middlesex
Polytechnic, 1971–73; Kingston
Polytechnic, 1973–79; Glasgow
University, and Parnham Trust,
1985–. External Assessor:
Middlesex Polytechnic, 1984–;
Royal College of Art, 1985–.
Member, Design Council Awards
Jury, 1980–.

Right: Cometa (kite) lamp,
designed 1972, in production
1976 by Disform, Barcelona;
and (sitting on the table) first
prototype of Tallo lamp,
later produced by b.d.
Barcelona. Both designed
with Charles Dillon.

Far right: Cometa lamp.

Jane Dillon is one of the few British furniture
designers working internationally in a freelance
capacity. She works on commercial (mainstream)
projects and shares a studio with Peter Wheeler and
Floris van den Broecke, both also furniture
designers. Her more experimental work however is
done independently, and it is this side of her work
that currently places her as an influential and
respected figure within avant garde trends in British
furniture design.

As to her background: Dillon received a Masters
degree in 1968 from the Royal College of Art, and for
a brief spell worked for Knoll International. Then an
important crossroad appeared in the form of two
concurrent offers. One presented the opportunity of
working with George Nelson in America, the other of
working with Ettore Sottsass at Olivetti in Italy. She
decided on Italy and became a consultant to Olivetti
Milan, collaborating with Sottsass on a project
concerned with office colouring and planning: in fact
one of the first design studies on the psychological
aspects of colour in the environment.

On returning to England in 1971, she married and
formed a partnership with Charles Dillon. In
addition to working in Britain at this time, they also
began developing projects in Barcelona, Spain – an
adventurous undertaking, initiated while Franco was
still alive and before Barcelona was recognised as an
international design centre. They continued to
conduct work in Barcelona on a regular basis for the
next ten years.

Jane Dillon's best known designs include the
'Cometa' lamp designed in 1971 (cometa is Spanish
for kite), and office chair ranges designed for Casas in
Barcelona – which are now Spain's best-selling
furniture export.

She has two children: Harry, aged 15 and Beatrice,
who is nine.

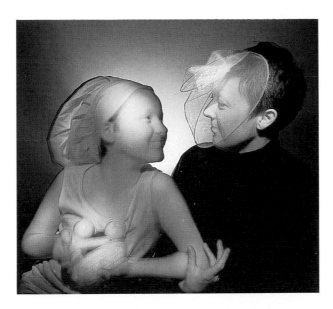

Right:
Jane Dillon and Beatrice

**Part of a conversation between Jane Dillon
and Floris van den Broeke,
taped at their studio in Clerkenwell, London**
*Floris van den Broeke is asking the questions*

*Was it objects or people that got you onto this road?*

I suppose it was people to begin with.

*Were those people involved in design?*

Not especially, but they were people who lived their lives with a
great deal of verve.

*Such as?*

My father was an architect and we lived for a good deal of the
time in a house he designed when he was in his early twenties.
It was quite magical for us as children and my parents' friends –
who came to the house – seemed very romantic and rather mad
compared to other people. There was always a tremendous
mixture of people and through them I somehow saw the world
quite differently – the way they behaved, the way they focused
their attention on certain things, the clothes they wore.

*Architecture is a very 'manly' profession dominated by male
architects . . . Do you see any connection between the building of
homes – and the building of houses and offices?*

Very strongly so, because objects and buildings are all in some
way to do with making a sense of place, and along with a sense
of place comes a sense of ceremony/ritual, codes of behaviour.
Objects like furniture locate and dictate the activity, the mood
and vice-versa. I remember my father saying many years ago
that he thought there was something wrong with design when a
Hertz Rent-a-Car waiting room looked and felt the same as a
modern church.

*But how can you as a designer deal with this?*

By being facinated by how and why people use objects and
spaces; perhaps by sometimes being sensitive to memories and
association. It's by thought patterns like this that I work.

*When and how did you realise that working in 3D was the right
thing to do?*

In my foundation year at Art School. I found being able to
model something easier than drawing it.

*Was there any particular awareness of being a woman?*

No, I have never been that conscious of my sex, although there have been moments in my professional life when I have been aware of being a woman – especially when in the company of men who were not used to working with a professional woman. I'm sure you will laugh and say I do nothing but chat up men!

*Well I think you chat up 3D objects!*

That's a nice way of putting it . . . I certainly do have a strong emotional response to objects.

*Yes, now is that something we could pin-point, because . . . it would be difficult to prove, but I have said many times that the best students are often women. But they are blocked in one way or another – overwhelmed, either by seeing the workshop full of machines, or by blokes bashing away with wood and metal and so on. Is that a problem that you have come across – the physicality of designing/making furniture?*

No, not really for me. As a student I suppose I was slightly arrogant . . . So when I saw the RCA workshop full of machines and blokes making things, my reaction was to turn my position around – believing that I was at an advantage. I had never physically handled wood, metal or machinery, and so was not hide-bound by all those mortice and tenon joints that they knew all about and could make so perfectly. So I went straight into thinking about ways around how to construct something. I also started to think about other aspects that might be involved . . . for example, 'chairness'.

*What I was trying to get you to talk about was that when it comes to working with 3D objects, women have a sensitivity to the design of objects that bashing away at bits of metal and wood does not.*

I think it is because there is a historical role in Britain of the 'Mr Fix It' (The Handy Man) who physically builds and mends things, that this male ego trip has often got in the way of a real sensitivity to the problem. I can give you a very good example of the 'handy man' at work. I remember asking Charles if he could make me a table to sew on. (He was 6ft 2in – I am 5ft 2in.) He came back with this fantastic solution: an immaculately-made board, faced with two coloured formica surfaces, beech-edged. It was 8ft × 4ft, so when I wanted to pick it up I couldn't even move it by myself. He did say it would be very useful for cutting out on! It seemed to be much more about his love of being able to glue an 8ft × 4ft sheet of formica down flat on a board without messing it up and edging it beautifully with beech, than about my problem – and that is what I mean. I feel rather nasty about using that as an example, because it was extremely well meant.

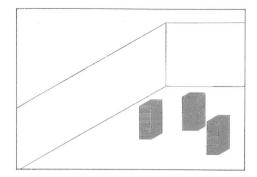
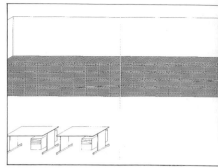

Above: Spreads from the book *The Art of Colouring the Office – Multiplication*, part of a project conducted in collaboration with Ettore Sottsass for Olivetti Milan, c.1969–71. The project was one of the first design studies on the psychological aspects of colour in the environment.

Right: 'Jobber' office chair range, started with partner Charles Dillon and finished after his death in 1982. Designed for Casas in Barcelona.

Right: The Wardrobe. (one of three versions)

'We (the West) live in a kind of nomadic state culturally and physically, often in a fantasy world manipulated by the media. The Wardrobe project was an attempt to find a balance between the memory of past, more permanent structures – large heavy wooden pieces of furniture with beautiful big decorated doors, full of strange smells of must and magic – and today's world of economic constraints'.

The Wardrobe is further explained in the caption on the right.

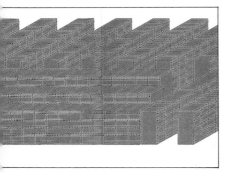

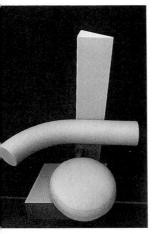

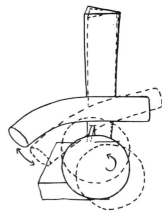

Left: Movable chair, designed 1967–68, produced by Planular/Italy, 1971.

A chair design which takes into account the constant movement, and many casual positions, of a seated person. There are 3 movable elements – a circular seat, a cylindrical backrest, and a supporting column; their movement in relation to one another provides varying support for the sitter. There is no one single axis. In addition, the complete seat is mounted on castors so that it can move about in space.

Left: The Wardrobe. (one of three versions)

Its structure consists of only a base housing a chassis, from which is supported a hanging rail, roof and two lightweight large aluminium doors. Although the wardrobe is lightweight, its presence in the room is substantial – even monumental, in the way old furniture is monumental. Nevertheless, it can be taken apart and reassembled, single-handedly. Lengths of silk are hung from the roof to form the walls, and provide flowing folds of material – harking back to the childhood memories of opening wardrobe doors and confronting flowing folds of material and clothing, strange smells etc . . . it is an extremely personal project.

*Your husband, whom you worked with, died five years ago. You have a heavy commitment to your family and quite a high profile working internationally. How do you manage it?*

You're beginning to sound like a Woman's Magazine! I think you know my output is actually quite small but I think it important to keep a reasonably high profile, even if (dare I say it) it means bull shitting. I say that only because until my children are old enough to be completely on their own, I want to give 50 percent of my time to them – therefore, consequently, the output is 50 percent less. I think the demand that children have on one is not something that gets turned on and off. It is constant, and it is that constant pull that makes continuity of thought and action extremely difficult, especially if you are quite slow at working as I am . . . slow in that I need to get really absorbed into the subject before I can get anything out at all that I feel happy with. Then I need fairly long periods of uninterrupted thought – from going to bed thinking about it, to getting up in the morning, to going to bed thinking about it again – and that I do not have and haven't had since having children 15 years ago.

*You have also taught a lot. Could you say something about that experience, particularly with reference to female students?*

The greatest difference in my experience between female and male students is that female students are much more private in their thoughts and often don't know how to translate these inner thoughts into their work.

*You have covered, very publicly, those various levels of expression, if you like . . You have worked on fairly anonymous projects that don't necessarily have a strong handwriting – and at the other end of the scale, very expressive objects which could not have been made or thought of by anybody else. How do you reconcile this – both in terms of style, and coming from one person?*

It is a little bit like buying a present in a way. If you know someone really well, for example, but they have a very different lifestyle and taste, you choose a present that suits them – the excitement is being able to be objective, to choose something that is just right for that person. The work that I did for Habitat comes in this category and the office chair ranges for Casas, Barcelona. There is a very fine line between just how much you can put of 'yourself' into it, and to what extent you choose ingredients that everybody else will like. Then there is the other part of my work which, if you want, is like making a nice present for me – but also knowing that there are quite a lot of people who like the same sort of things I do. To do something that reaches a broad audience is important, but without pandering to that audience. The work for me has to have interest, intensity and integrity – without these there is no point to work.

# Prudence Fenton *animation*

**Biography**
Educated at: Vassar College,
New York, BA Independent
major, architecture and
journalism, 1971–75; Corcoran
School of Art, Washington DC,
BFA and Ford Foundation Grant
for institutional mural, 1977–81.
Worked for Broadcast Arts Inc,
Washington DC, 1981–84, as
Associate Producer, Sound/Film
Editor and Office Manager.
Joined Peter Wallach Enterprises
Inc, New York, in 1985 as
Producer, Production Manager
and Editor; produced
commercials and rock videos for,
amongst others, MGM,
Wendy's, and RC Cola. Line
Producer for Peter Gabriel's rock
video 'Big Time', 1986. Rejoined
Broadcast Arts Inc, in New
York, 1986 and produced
commercial campaigns for
McDonald's and Visine, and the
animation for the ABC pilot
'Wayside School'. Then Senior
Animation Producer of the new
CBS series 'Pee-wee's Playhouse'
(Broadcast Arts Inc, 1986).
Animation and Effects Producer
for second season of 'Pee-wee's
Playhouse' (BRB Productions,
Los Angeles, 1987). In 1982
received ASIFA Award for
design of MTV program ID
'Pink Elephant'; and in 1987 she
received an Emmy Award for
outstanding achievement in
graphics and title design for 'Pee-
wee's Playhouse'.

Prudence Fenton has been responsible for the animation and special effects of two seasons of 'Pee-wee's Playhouse', a Saturday morning children's programme shown on national network television in America (1986 and 1987); she received an Emmy Award for the design of the show's opening titles in 1986. She has also produced IDs (animated logos) for MTV, rock videos, and a large number of television commercials. In the following notes she describes her varied background and her even more varied work experiences:

## Background

'I grew up in Greenville, Delaware, a town where careers in business and law were respected and understood, but careers in art and design were viewed with skepticism. Women were expected to raise families and support the husband's career, perhaps dabbling in real estate on the side.

I was always interested in forms of visual expression. In my high school years I thought that the only accepted career I could have in a visual field would be as an architect. I wanted very much to go to art school, but at the urging of my family I went instead to Vassar College as my sister had. I designed a major that combined architecture with English, but I left college with no clear sense of direction.

After college, I went to Houston, Texas to work for my brother, a real estate developer who was turning a Boy Scout campsite into expensive single-family homes. There I learned the practical realities of designing and building houses. I became disillusioned with the role of the architect and went to live in West Texas where I worked for the local Odessa newspaper writing vanity pieces for the business section. I started doing cartooning and mechanical illustrations for the local tool companies. I realized that I could find work in the visual arts, but a formal art education was necessary.

At this point I managed to convince my parents that I was beginning a practical career that required an art education to pursue. I chose the Corcoran School of Art in Washington DC. They emphasized classical skills like drawing, painting and sculpture; coincidentally, my grandmother had also gone there in the late 1800s.

For four years I concentrated on drawing and sculpting. In the last two years I developed a cartoon character called Arthur Byrd. At the suggestion of a curator at the Smithsonian, I taught myself how to animate my character; no courses in animation were taught at the Corcoran. I made several Super-Eight films and showed them to the three local animation companies in town. I did not land an animation job immediately.

After graduation, I began my career in the film industry as a gopher for the fledgling animation firm Broadcast Arts. We animated objects, photos or clay characters in miniature sets and used cel animation for enhancement. We called ourselves a mixed-media operation.

These beginnings had a considerable influence on me. I became familiar with a wide variety of unusual materials and methods. At various times, I worked in every conceivable job in that tiny but ambitious studio. I was in charge of getting the film processed overnight, usually via courier in NYC but sometimes as far away as Canada on weekends. I came up with an award-winning concept for one MTV ID, created and edited sound effects, painted cells, ran the camera or did stop-motion animation in gruelling 10 and 15-hour sessions. Eventually, I worked my way up from production assistant to assistant producer, and finally got a chance to produce commercial spots from start to finish, including budgeting and client contact.

I moved to NYC to be in one of the best places for animation artists and work. At first, I was with another animation studio, Peter Wallach. But soon, Broadcast Arts moved to NYC too and I rejoined them for several projects. My most notable achievement was production of animation and special effects for "Pee-wee's Playhouse". I was invited to move to Los Angeles to work on the second season, and while there won an Emmy award for the design of the show's opening titles in 1986.

### Areas of involvement

There are three main sides to animated film production: the design aspect, the technical side and most importantly the team or crew that does the work.

*The design:* What I find so exciting about animation is that anything can be animated; any reality is possible and one is never limited to a specific "look". Any material, texture or shape can be designed, manipulated, incremented, filmed and brought to life.

One of our first design problems at Broadcast Arts was to create animated MTV IDs. Some of the most creative animation on television was being done in these tiny segments. We were allowed to animate practically anything for 10 seconds, as long as when 8 seconds had elapsed, the MTV logo had appeared. I won a design award from ASIFA for a Pink Elephant that turns into the MTV logo. He snorts up some flowers, squirts them onto his leg to make the "TV" and then he transforms into a giant "M".

In all, we did about 20 MTV logos. We made an MTV sandwich. We had a bathroom setting where a Hairy M was breathing; a can of shaving cream cruises by and squirts the TV part on the M. There was an M that fell to earth like a meteorite. TV sets fell from the sky to form the MTV. We melted an iced form of MTV and showed it in reverse.

For commercial jobs, we distorted skis, melted houses, made people cry inside dollar bills that were melting. Microphones sang, lips ate, cars winked. All were made of different materials depending on the technique we used and the style the client wanted, and the action of the piece.

*The technical side:* The technical aspect influences the design and often dictates the materials used, and to a certain degree can set the style. Much of how something is done depends on the equipment available and how much money is in the budget.

*The team:* The people who execute the production are very crucial. A director I used to work with said that the best preparation for the film world would be a degree in psychology. You can never predict who is going to cause trouble or get along well.

Keeping the team balanced and moving forward is what I try to do. It is not easy to "design" the team; in fact, it is often a crap shoot. Some combinations of people can produce stupendous results and others can produce disasters. There can be negative situations and good results. There is no formula; each project is unique, and it is always interesting to examine the string of decisions that produces a successful, completed job.

There are three titles used to define my current work position: Producer, Director of Effects, or Artistic Manager. My responsibilities include budgeting, hiring, managing the staff, being the liaison between creatives, directing critiquing, post-production and seeing the project through to completion.

Above: Prudence Fenton

**Most difficult project**

In November of 1986 I was asked to do a rock video for Peter Gabriel. I had to find a production house in NYC, do the budget, get it designed and completed in 16 days. What was most significant for me was that I was in charge of everything. There was no-one or company above me. I could succeed – or I could really hang myself. In reality, it was a nightmare.

The design was way too ambitious for the time allotted. Much of it was too technique-oriented; animation for animation's sake. Several shots just did not work, but the overall piece was dazzling; it was a song about the BIG TIME and what happens to people when they get to the BIG TIME and the video to a certain degree reflected the lyrics. Everyone working on the job suffered burn out, and I don't believe it is ever worth it to stretch myself or anybody else that far again.

I learned that I could do the impossible, but there is more to creating art/visuals or animation than that. It is very important to give ideas time to grow and change, and be refined. There is an important process involved that cannot be condensed.

The "Big Time" video changed the way I think about the production process; I prefer to work on longer term projects and really take the time to make the vision whole.'

Far left: Beauty Contest, Life in the Fridge, Pee-wee's Playhouse, 1987.

Left: Life in the Fridge, Pee-wee's Playhouse, 1987.

Right: 8 Arms to Hold You video, Peter Wallach Enterprises, New York City, 1985.

Right: The Bread Group, Pee-wee's Playhouse, 1987.

Above: Mr RC Cola, Peter
Wallach Enterprises, New
York City, 1984.

Left: Mr Ham's Surprise
Birthday Party, Life in the
Fridge, Pee-wee's Playhouse,
1987.

43

# Britain

# June Fraser *graphic and industrial design*

**Biography**
Born 1930 in United Kingdom.
Educated at: Royal College of
Art, London, Associate of Royal
College of Art (ARCA), 1957.
President of Chartered Society of
Designers, 1983–85; Member of
the Institute of Packaging,
1973–. Awards: European
Packaging Prize, 'Eurostar',
1962; DRU design award, 1963;
'Star' Design Award for Astralux
Cartons (for Hoskyns Group Ltd
Computer Software), 1970; Irish
Glass Award (DE Williams
liqueur bottles), 1973. Design
experience: Design Research
Unit, 1957–80 (Partner – 1963,
Director – DRU Ltd, 1968);
Head of Graphic Design, John
Lewis Partnership, 1980–84;
Head of Industrial Design, The
Design Council, 1984–. Work
exhibited internationally and
shown in numerous books and
magazines. Appointments: Hon
Treasurer and Vice President,
SIAD, 1979–81; President,
SIAD, 1983–85; Council
Member, The Design Council,
1984; DIA Board Member,
1985–87; Product Design Review
Advisory Board (Building
Products), 1985; Member of the
Court, Royal College of Art,
London, 1986; Governor, The
London Institute, 1986;
Governor, Bournemouth & Poole
College of Art, 1986;
International Board of ICSID,
1987. Married to Allen Cull (also
a designer/teacher), daughter Zoe
born in 1970.

Below: June Fraser

Known for her work in the past as head of graphic design at Design Research Unit and again at John Lewis Partnership, June Fraser has in recent years undertaken leadership roles of broader significance to the British design community. From 1983 to 1985 she served as the elected President of the Chartered Society of Designers (the designers' professional body) and in 1984 became Head of Industrial Design at the Design Council, charged with the important mission of promoting the cause of design to British industry . . .

'My present job at The Design Council is as Head of the Industrial Design Division and I am one of the four strong directorate of the Design Council. I am responsible for three main activities each of which has a manager who reports to me.

*Design Centre Selection:* The Design Council black and white label scheme which selects the best products "from the High Street" and awards them the black and white label.

*The Designers Register:* A register of 1600+ designers in product, fashion/textile, graphics and interior design whom we recommend to industry.

*Exhibitions:* The design and administration of Design Council exhibitions held in the Centre at Haymarket and touring exhibitions all over the UK, and occasionally overseas.

I am also Editor in Chief of *Design* Magazine, which seeks to tell industry and commerce about design and designers. The Design Council's office in Cardiff is also under my direction.

In addition I am responsible for the graphic/industrial design standards of all activities in the Council, eg. shop, videos, literature, annual report etc.

I am also required to have an input on industrial design education.

**Previous positions**
Although trained as a graphic designer my interest has always been in three-dimensional design. The third dimension became increasingly expressed in my work through packaging.

When I left the Royal College of Art my aim was to work in a multi-disciplinary practice and Design Research Unit (Misha Black/Milner Gray) was the goal. I got my first job there having turned down a job with Lyons Packaging. Professor Guyatt at the

RCA was dismayed that I had turned it down because the salary was too little, which suggested that we were lucky to be offered jobs at all!

My first success at DRU was an animation for ABC Television, for which I also directed the all-electronic music composed by Tristram Carey. The first packaging success came when I won a Starpack Award, followed by a European packaging prize "Eurostar", for Berkshire hosiery packaging. It was the first time that a pack half the size of the conventional one was used and a first for the use of PVC in packaging. But all these innovations would have been useless had the girls in the factory in Northern Ireland been unable to pack the stockings into half-size packs with the same speed.

In 1963 I redesigned Wedgwood's logotype and corporate identity and their range of gift boxes. It has remained on the market ever since – a record 24 years.

One of my toughest jobs was to do a pack for a computer software programme; an indefinable number of cards, a requirement to have flat packs for storage and a cosmetic treatment. It won an award.

In the mid 1960s and early 1970s I worked on several large corporate identities, where the teams often consisted of an architect, interior designer and myself. Jobs such as these were the ones I enjoyed most, when I was working with people at all levels of a company to achieve solutions which involved more than just surface graphics.

Inevitably working in one company as I did for so long, means that as you get near the top of the organisation you gradually do less design, the very reason for which you were originally employed. After Milner Gray retired I took over the graphic side of DRU's practice and soon found that I was getting work only for others to enjoy doing it. In 1980 I resigned and joined the John Lewis Partnership to get back to the drawing board.

The four years I spent at the John Lewis Partnership were some of the busiest, most educative and most frustrating I have ever known. I completed a huge amount of work with one fully-trained assistant (who came with me from DRU) and an inherited team, half of whom had been very badly trained, if at all. Not only did we redesign all the Jonelle own-brand packaging – everything from children's clothes to paints – but wine and spirit labels for Waitrose, and some non-food packaging as well. I was forbidden to get any publicity for my work at all: it was one of the Partnership's puritanical rules that one did not promote oneself.

By the end of 1983 I was getting restless. Most of the department store work had been done and I was pressing the Directors to extend their brand's horizon into specially designed furniture, household equipment, fashion etc. In fact I was dying to get out of the graphic box to which I was permanently chained within the Partnership. Early in 1984, I was head-hunted for my present job and escaped to the wider horizons of The Design Council.

## Reflections

Most of my design work is practical, cost effective and economical in the use of materials. I have always believed in straightforward solutions and the jobs I have enjoyed most have been those where I had to be ingenious within tight cost parameters. Many products fail because the market for them has been ill-defined and insufficient thought has been given to what the consumer really wants or the convenience of use. If people like a product they will buy it. If they find a pack attractive enough to pick up, a purchase is usually always made. Cost is not the major factor in making a decision to buy. A product may be excellent in all respects but if it does not have visual appeal it will not move off the shelf. A good analogy is that of a car – a person buying a car assumes it will be well-engineered, but they buy mainly on its looks and what it will say about their lifestyle, and it is the industrial designer who provides that.

## Women in design

In my experience women bring a unique contribution to any design job; they are more sensitive, intuitive and imaginative, which usually enables them to go straight to a solution without having to resort to reams of writing to justify it all. They do not have the ego problems which many men have so it is easier for them to admit they are wrong and they have the unique ability to put themselves in their clients' position. They are more practical than men, better listeners and able to establish better working relationships. Their ability to rush from job to job at home means that they accomplish far more at a certain level, though I think women often lack the time to think a problem out at length and this denies some of them the success they deserve.'

Above: Waitrose Ltd, labels for own-brand wines/spirits; (left) a range of French wines, and (right) Italian wines and an Alsace wine; designed with Mark Smith, 1981.

Above: Symbol for Slinger Group of Companies; based on an S, 1965.

Left: John Lewis Partnership, own-brand packaging for Jonelle (the oven foil packaging is shown here), 1983.

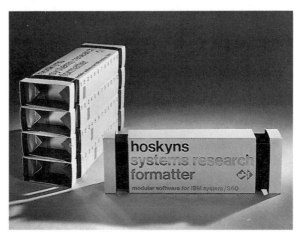

Left: Hoskyns Systems Research, Unit Packs for modular software (to be used in IBM computers); designed primarily for the American market. The unit packs each hold 200 punched cards, and are assembled in multiples to house programs of up to 2,500 cards. Each program is packed in an outer carton with four instruction manuals. The unit packs and outer cartons are designed to be stored flat, for assembly by the client.

Winner of the Astralux Carton Award, 1970.

# Nicolete Gray *writing and research on lettering*

**Biography**
Born 1911 in England. Educated at: Oxford University, reading History; British School of Rome, as a scholar, studying Dark Age inscriptions, 1931. Teacher of Lettering, Central School of Art and Design, 1964–1981. Married to Basil Gray; they had five children. Publications: books – *Nineteenth Century Ornamented Typefaces*, Faber & Faber, London, 1938, revised 1986; *Lettering as drawing: the moving line*, Oxford University Press, 1970; *Lettering as drawing: contour and silhouette*, Oxford University Press, 1970; *Lettering on Buildings*, 1960; *The Painted Inscriptions of David Jones*, Gordon Fraser, London, 1981; *A history of lettering: creative experiment and letter identity*, Phaidon Press, Oxford, 1986; selected articles – 'The Civic Trust and Lettering', *Typographica 4*, Lund Humphries, London, December 1961; 'Lettering in Coventry Cathedral', *Typographica 6*, Lund Humphries, London, December 1962; 'Lettering and Society', *Visible Language*, Vol 8 No 3, The MIT Press, Cambridge, Mass, Summer 1974, pp247–260.

Nicolete Gray's books on the artistic and expressive aspects of lettering have influenced generations of art and design students and professionals in Britain. Her writings span a period of nearly fifty years, and refuse to fade in their appeal. More than anyone in Britain, she has promoted lettering as a branch of art history, and also as a 'living' subject for students in art schools. Her well known book *Lettering as Drawing* (an aesthetic analysis) is now considered a classic work; *Nineteenth Century Ornamented Typefaces*, originally published in 1938 then revised and expanded in 1986, has caused many a present-day typography student to swerve from the Modernist line and venture in search of a more eccentric typographic past. But the appeal is not solely to do with the subject material; it is also a delight for the reader to confront extensive research delivered in such a congenial tone. These are books to learn from, and to enjoy . . . they breathe love of the subject.

As to her own past, Nicolete Gray was educated at Oxford, reading history, and went as a scholar to the British School of Rome in 1931 where she studied Dark Age inscriptions. She married Basil Gray, and they had five children.

Gray describes herself as being mainly a writer of books on lettering; these include *Lettering on Buildings* 1960, *Lettering as Drawing* 1971, *A History of Lettering* 1986, and *Nineteenth Century Ornamented Typefaces* 1938, 1986. She was also a teacher of lettering at the Central School of Art and Design in London from 1964 to 1981.

Gray's design work is solely to do with lettering (she stresses that she is *not* a calligrapher) and has been mainly carving in stone, although she has also carved in wood and designed for mosaic. She works on her own and states that although she had minimal art school training, her extensive study of letter-forms of the past has been a real advantage. She expresses particular interest in three-dimensional and superimposed forms, and in experimental and expressionist possibilities.

Above: Nicolete Gray working on the Stratford inscription.

Right and far right: Spreads from the book *Nineteenth Century Ornamented Typefaces*, published in 1938.

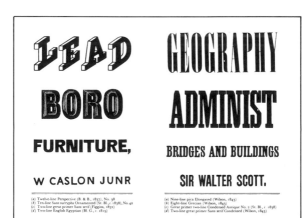

LEAD

BORO

FURNITURE,

W CASLON JUNR

(a) Twelve-line Perspective (B. & B., 1837), No. 38
(b) Ten-line Sans turrypha Ornamented (St. Bl., c. 1838), No. 42
(c) Two-line great primer Sans serif (Figgins, 1832)
(d) Two-line English Egyptian (Bl. G., c. 1819)

GEOGRAPHY

ADMINIST

BRIDGES AND BUILDINGS

SIR WALTER SCOTT.

(a) Nine-line pica Elongated (Wilson, 1843)
(b) Eight-line Grecian (Wilson, 1843)
(c) Great primer two-line Condensed Antique No. 2 (St. Bl., c. 1838)
(d) Two-line great primer Sans serif Condensed (Wilson, 1843)

Above: Wall panel at the Shakespeare Memorial Library, Stratford on Avon, 1962; executed on wood, panels of different woods being superimposed on one another; some letters in relief, others cut through into different woods. The design, incorporating the names of Shakespeare and his contemporaries, expresses their differences in work and stature.

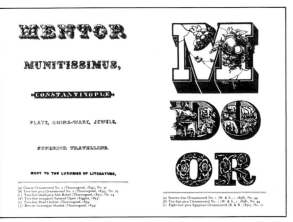

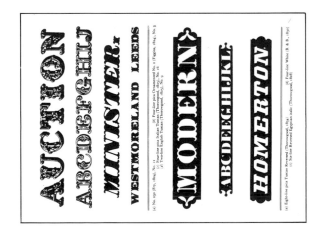

# USA   April Greiman *graphic design*

**Biography**
Born 1948 in New York, USA.
Educated at: Kansas City Art
Institute, BFA, 1970; Allgemeine
Kunstgewerbeschule, Basle,
graduate studies, 1970–71.
Clients include: Esprit; Xerox
Corporation; Los Angeles Times;
1984 Los Angeles Olympic
Committee; Optica; Benetton;
Inference Corporation; Sebastian
International; and many others –
also film and television
companies, record companies,
magazines, schools, museums
and art galleries, and individuals.
Designed magazine covers for:
*Interiors*, June 1987; *PC World*,
Feb 1987; *Los Angeles Times
Calendar Magazine*, Dec 1984;
*Progressive Architecture*, Sept
1983; *Idea*, No 179, July 1983;
*Wet*, July and Sept 1979; *Art
Direction*, July 1978. Professional
affiliations: Alliance Graphique
Internationale; AIGA, National
Board Member; AIGA, Los
Angeles, Vice President; Art
Directors Club, Los Angeles;
STA, Chicago; Type Directors
Club, New York.

California's image as the land of the wierd and wonderful provides a suitable backdrop for one of America's most innovative graphic designers, April Greiman.

Greiman studied at Kansas City Art Institute in the late 1960s, and in the early 1970s received further training at the Allgemeine Kunstgewerbeschule in Basle, the home of 'Swiss graphics'. On return from Basle, Greiman worked professionally in New York then in 1977 moved to the West Coast. There she quickly emerged as a leading figure in New Wave graphic design.

The unique quality of her work stems from the combining of the Swiss ethic and its obsessive concern for structure and order, with her own painterly collage-sense and California colouring. Through the layering of colour, texture, language and fragmented imagery, her collages come alive with the buzz and complexity of modern life . . . chaos that is expertly controlled.

Greiman's best known projects from the New Wave period include the publicity material she created for California Institute of the Arts in collaboration with photographer Jayme Odjers; 'Spacemats' – table placemats for visually aware people; and designs for *WET*, a magazine of gourmet bathing.

The early 1980s found her as program director of Visual Communication at California Institute of the Arts (1982–84), and embarking on explorations into three-dimensional design in the form of interiors and furniture. Her present fascinations are for new technology and video graphics. The Apple Macintosh computer is presently one of Greiman's most valued tools, and she involves it in her work in virtually every stage of the design process, from conceptualising to realisation. An example of the power of the Macintosh influence can be seen in a special issue of *Design Quarterly* magazine (no. 133), which she designed using various Macintosh programs. The issue is titled 'Does it make sense?' and unfolds to become a 2ft × 6ft poster incorporating a computerised word and image collage, as well as carrying an explanatory essay on how the project was conceived, developed and finally printed.

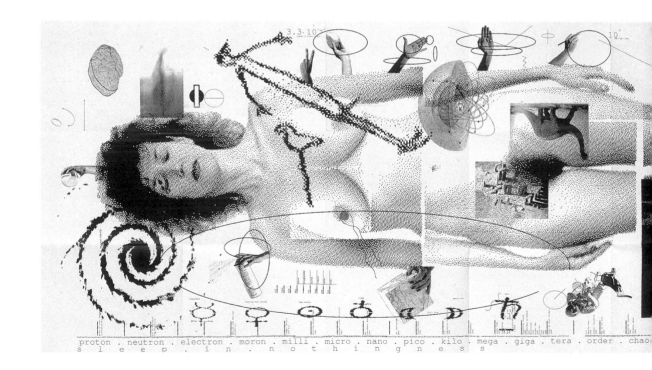

Poster, Workspace, 1987.

April Greiman

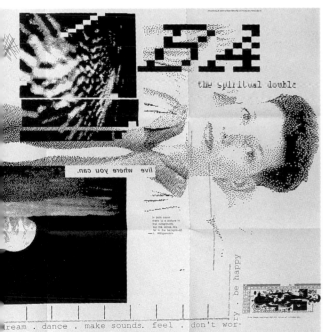

Left: Poster fold-out
(2ft x 6ft), *Design Quarterly*
No. 133, 1986.

# Britain

# Zaha Hadid *architecture*

**Biography**
Born 1950 in Baghdad, Iraq.
Educated at: American
University of Beirut, degree in
Mathematics, 1971;
Architectural Association School
of Architccture, London, AA
Diploma Prize, 1977. Joined
Office for Metropolitan
Architecture, 1977. Commenced
teaching at the Architectural
Association (with R Koolhaas
and E Zenghelis), 1977.
Commenced private practice in
London, 1980. Projects include:
Apartments, London, 1985; New
Furniture, London, and IBA
Housing, Berlin, 1986. Has
lectured internationally.
Visiting Design Critic at:
Harvard Graduate School of
Design, 1986, and Columbia
University NYC, 1987. Awards:
Gold Medal, AD British
Architecture Awards for an
apartment conversion, Eaton
Place, London, 1982; First Prize

at 'The Peak' International
Competition, Hong Kong, 1983;
winning entry for the
Kurfürstendamm Office Building
(competition), Berlin, 1986. Has
exhibited in galleries and
museums worldwide. Selected
publications and further reading:
Z. Hadid, *Planetary Architecture
Two*, (folio of work), Z. Hadid
and the Architectural
Association, London, 1983;
Yukio Futagawa (ed.), *GA
Architect: Zaha M. Hadid*, ADA
Edita, Tokyo, 1986.

Above: Zaha Hadid

Architect Zaha Hadid and her team currently practice in the converted studio of a Victorian schoolhouse in Clerkenwell, London. The team numbers up to five or six people, depending on the nature of the job in hand, and is a mixture of designers, painters and architects. The atmosphere is one of studious calm; the impact of their work on the architectural scene in recent years has been anything but that.

In 1983 Zaha Hadid shot to worldwide attention with her winning design for 'The Peak' competition in Hong Kong: an international competition for the design of a private club and residential complex on a cliff site overlooking Hong Kong, which drew 600 entries from around the world. Winning the event provided a fair amount of thunder in itself, but she also succeeded in rattling the architectural establishment to its very core with the innovative nature of her design.

Claiming early Suprematist exercises for its roots, her approach extends beyond present conventions of architectural arrangement and composition, and develops a new direction of its own. She confronts us with the notion that social and technological changes demand new ways of living and working, new uses of spaces, new attitudes to planning our built environment – in short, a new vision.

To describe this new vision she incorporates radical methods of representation. Designs are developed through paintings, architectural drawings, concept diagrams, sketches, models and studies. These become an expression of the various 'lives' and qualities of a building (time of day, location, environmental colouring etc), while also examining and presenting the building from every possible angle: hence the use of bird's-eye views and worm's-eye views.

The result is a storytelling process of a sort . . . that engulfs and overwhelms the viewer. For the visual language involved is one of shifting planes, distorted perspective, and dynamic movement – with an overriding feeling of liberating energy, often described as explosive. (And the paintings and drawings range from hand-size to 4ft × 8ft!). Buildings are no longer seen as static objects, but the embodiment of a space/time continuum; a vibrating, animated extension of human life. Liberation is the key concept in the storytelling, and a powerful and optimistic force it is. The storytelling is also soundly

based in reality, for the structural feasibility of every project is worked out in conjunction with the distinguished engineering firm of Ove Arup & Partners.

The next phase of the adventure is soon to begin. Hadid's schemes to date have existed solely as proposals; now the vision becomes a reality. Two buildings in West Berlin have received planning permission: one is a residential block (part of a housing scheme) for IBA – Internationale Bauausstellung, Berlin – which is due to begin construction next year; and the other is a small office building on the Kurfürstendamm. In addition, two new buildings in Tokyo are scheduled to begin on site within a year.

Zaha Hadid's present team consists of Michael Wolfson, Brenda MacKneson, Nicky Cousins, and Andrew King.

Below: Site plan for Grand Buildings Project

**Trafalgar Square
Grand Buildings Project**
London 1985
(competition entry)

Due to the convention of perimeter building, London's Trafalgar Square has become reduced to the status of a traffic island – sealed in by a circular traffic route and alienated from the public. Maintaining that such ideas about site planning are no longer appropriate, Hadid approaches the problem in a totally new way. The project shown here involves a complex of buildings, located on the south side of the square, and explores the possibilities of extending public territory into the office/work domain. The complex includes a slab of offices, a shopping concourse, parking, restaurant and entertainment facilities, and features a peripheral ramp (for public access) offering spectacular views of Trafalgar Square. General facilities and spacial areas such as terraces exist for use simultaneously by both the public and the office workers. Through its concern for the mixing of two worlds, the project explores the important issue of how modern architecture can make a contribution to the quality of urban living.

Grand Buildings team:
Michael Wolfson
Brian Ma-Siy
Kar-Hwa Ho
Piers Smerin
Nicky Cousins
David Gomersall
Nan Lee
Madelaine Palme

Below: View of site with London skyline

**Trafalgar Square Grand Buildings Project**

Right: Night view of slab block, rear elevation.

Below: In the slab/tower: interior of office-scape, and floor planes.

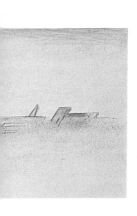

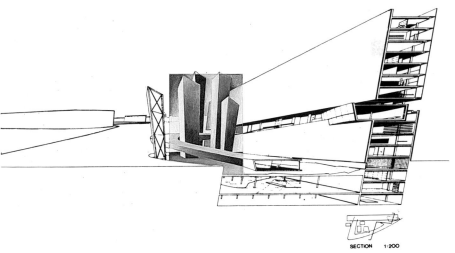

Left: Section/perspective.

Below: Worm's eye view of ramp and towers, with movement diagrams (showing the building rotating).

SECTION 1:200

# Britain

# Ruhi Hamid *graphic design*

**Biography**
Born 1956 in Mwanza, Tanzania. Educated at: Middlesex Polytechnic, England, BA Graphic Design, 1980; Royal College of Art, London, MA Graphic Information Design, 1983. During her studies, worked with: Fulcrum (Design Consultants) London, June–August 1980; Total Design, Amsterdam, Holland, August 1982 and September–December 1983. After graduating, worked with Studio Dumbar in The Hague, 1984–85, and with the Maviyane Project in Harare, Zimbabwe, 1985–86. Returned to Britain in 1986. Continued working as a freelance designer. Part-time teaching in various art schools in Britain. Awards: 'The Other Book' Award, London Book Fair, for *Tales of Mozambique*, Young World Books, 1980; Bronze Medal, 11th Brno Biennial of Graphic Design, Czechoslovakia, 1984; Gold Award, Netherlands Design and Art Directors club, 1986; Gold Award, Design and Art Directors Club, Great Britain, for design of signage system for the Rijksmuseum Amsterdam (with Gert Dumbar and Michel de Boer), 1987. Exhibitions: Third World Biennial of Graphic Art, London, 1980; Third World Artists' Co-operative, University of London, 1981; Third World Art Exhibition, London School of Economics, 1981; First Festival of Progressive African Art, London, 1981; Seven Black Graduates, Royal College of Art, London, 1983; Brno Biennial of Graphic Design, Czechoslovakia, 1984 and 1986; Inter-Graphic 84, Poster Biennial, Berlin, 1984; Lahti Poster Biennial, Finland, 1985 and 1987; 11th Poster Biennial, Warsaw, 1986; Design and Art Directors Club Annual, The Netherlands, 1986; Design and Art Directors Club, Annual, Great Britain, 1986. Currently working at the BBC, London, in the department of TV News Graphics.

Ruhi Hamid was born in Tanzania of Asian origin, and later educated in Britain. The combining of an Asian and African background has had a profound influence on her life and work: 'The motivation in my design career and in my life – what makes me "tick" – has always arisen from my commitment to my cultural and political background. Coming from the developing world . . . I feel one has a responsibility to contribute to the progress and advancement of the developing world.' The need to explore and be in touch with third world cultures has caused her to travel extensively over the past ten years, visiting Mexico, Guatemala, Turkey, Pakistan, Northern India, and East and South African countries.

Now aged 31, Ruhi Hamid's career to date has moved at a fast pace. Hamid studied graphic design in London and received a Masters degree from the Royal College of Art in 1983, specialising in educational information design. She then took on a position at Studio Dumbar in Holland and during her two-year stay there played a major role in the design of an award-winning sign system for the Rijksmuseum Amsterdam.

Armed with professional experience she wished to put to use in the developing world, she travelled to Zimbabwe in 1985 and joined the Maviyane Project in Harare. The Maviyane Project consisted of a team of three designers and one photographer, dedicated to the idea of challenging the type of design and visual imagery produced by the white-dominated advertising industry (which they felt patronised the black community). She worked there for just over a year on assorted projects such as *Moto* magazine, which dealt with current social and political issues in Zimbabwe and the rest of the world, and the book *Another Battle Begun* which covered the Co-operative Movement's plan to integrate the guerilla fighters from the Rhodesian War back into society (the new, independent socialist state of Zimbabwe) by teaching them new skills.

Feeling that the developing world was in need of professional skills she still lacked, Hamid travelled back to England and is now working with the BBC. After gaining sufficient experience, she intends to return once again to Africa to develop the use of television as an educational tool, working within a local station.

Ruhi Hamid on the way to Botswana by train, 1986.

*Moto* magazine cover, Zimbabwe, 1986.

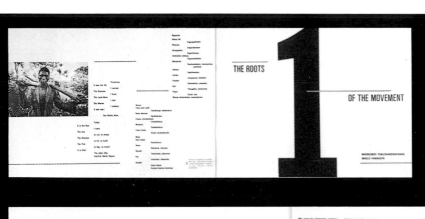

Cover (above) and spreads from *Another Battle Begun*, a book on the Co-operative Movement in Zimbabwe; with photographer Bruce Paton, 1985.

# Japan
# Itsuko Hasegawa *architecture*

**Biography**
Born 1941 in Yaizu City, Japan.
Educated at: The School of
Architecture, Kanto-gakuin
University, graduated, 1963;
studied at Kazuo Shinohara
laboratory, Tokyo Institute of
Technology, 1969–71. Worked
at: Kiyonori Kikutake, Architect
and Associates, 1964–69; Kazuo
Shinohara laboratory, Tokyo
Institute of Technology, 1971–
76. Established Itsuko Hasegawa
Architectural Design Studio,
1976. Works include: House 1 in
Yaizu, Shizuoka, 1972; House in
Kamoi, Kanagawa, 1975; House
in Midorigaoka, Tokyo, 1975;
House 2 in Yaizu, Shizuoka,
1977; House in Kakio, Tokyo,
1977; Stationery Shop in Yaizu,
Shizuoka, 1978; Tokumaru
Children's Clinic, Ehime, 1979;
House in Kuwabara,
Matsuyama, Ehime, 1980; Aono
Building, Ehime, 1982; House in
Itami, Osaka, 1982; House in
Kanazawabunko, Kanagawa,
1983; NC House, Tokyo, 1984;
Bizan Hall, Shizuoka, 1984;
House in Ikebukuro, Tokyo,
1984; House in Oyama, Tochigi,
1985; Work M (Project), 1985;
BY House, Tokyo, 1985; House
in Kumamoto, 1986; House in
Nerima, Tokyo, 1986; Atelier in
Tomigaya, Tokyo, 1986; Sugai
Internal Clinic, Ehime, 1986;
House in Higashi-Tamagawa,
Tokyo, 1986; MN House
(Project), Tokyo, 1987; KK
House, Tokyo, 1987; Shonandai
Cultural Center, 1987–.

Cosmic forces, change of season, freedom of the human spirit . . these are some of the concepts embodied in the work of Japanese architect Itsuko Hasegawa, in her on-going development of the idea of 'naturalness'.

Residential design forms a central part of her work. Much of it has been small, low-cost housing (for families with below median incomes – normally neglected by architects) although more recently she has undertaken apartment and multi-purpose buildings, as well as public and community centres. Her largest work to date is the Shonandai Cultural Center at Fujisawa, a commission she obtained by winning a national competition in 1986. The building, designed as a 'topography' of environmental and cosmic elements, is currently under construction, and the first phase should be completed in 1989.

The following excerpts are from an article by Hasegawa[1] in which she describes the Asian influence in her work, and her concern about the urban environment.

'The philosophy of *feng-shui*, which seeks to engage nature in the guise of light, wind, earth, water and fire, informs the architectural ideas of Asia. Moreover, these ideas reflect the belief that human spiritual activities are also a part of the natural process and that architecture is a product of the human spirit, or rather of spiritual refinement. To be in a natural state means to be in a place that is invigorating, flexible and spacious, a place where consciousness flows freely. This Asian quality has been brutally destroyed or forcibly transformed by that structural philosophy called modernization. Certainly this has been true in architecture, from which many things have been excluded and in which a quality increasingly antithetical to nature prevails. Matters of great importance that had formed unbroken chains have been interrupted, for example, the cosmic and religious quality that existed in the mountains, the sea and the shrines, the diversity and fluidity that enabled an agrarian society to coexist with other living things, the mysterious and symbolic quality that was generated by an engagement with nature, and the mazelike quality and neighborhood territoriality of villages and towns . . .

I live in a district that is an extension of the crowded residential area located below the skyscrapers in the West Shinjuku subcenter of Tokyo. I am right in the midst of a mixture of the old and the new. In the distance stand tall buildings shining in the sunrise or sunset and illuminated at night, and all around me are houses where old customs are maintained and where the changes of the seasons are appreciated. Even in my neighborhood there are a number of things about which I am concerned. Along the street, there used to flow a little stream that restored one's calm, and stone statues of *jizō* (a bodhisattva) stood without any great ceremony and prompted one to make a prayer. It was fun to walk on the street. Now, however, unwieldy guardrails divide pedestrian zones from vehicular lanes, and signs hinder and endanger pedestrians. Soft, easily drained paths for the aged and the young, and paths for wheelchairs and bicycles ought to be provided, but everything is paved in the same manner as vehicular lanes. The hedges of azalea along the sidewalk seem extensions of the all too artificial greenery that is found around the bases of skyscrapers. Why can't greenery distinctive to the area be planted? It isn't just mothers who are raising children that are concerned; everyone wants to live in an environment in which he or she can be aware of the changes of the season . . .

I architecturalize images of nature because I want to express a view of the contemporary world – one that sees the potential for living in greater freedom. I use architectural and technological details to evoke nature and natural and cosmic details to evoke architecture. I am coming to feel that the issue of the autonomy of architecture must be explored from an entirely new direction if we are to attain a flexible and spatious naturalness and freedom.'

Above: Itsuko Hasegawa

[1] '3 Projects', *The Japan Architect*, Nov/Dec 1986, pp54–5.

## House in Nerima

'Despite its convenient location relative to transporation to the center of the city, this is a relatively underdeveloped residential area. To maintain the favorable conditions with regard to sunlight, natural ventilation, and privacy, was the aim of design. Many parts of the plan of this house were patterned after the client's previous house, a delicate task of fitting the house to the client's acquired set of living habits. The structure is composed of the main part of the house for the couple who are novelists and the living quarters of their daughter. Between these two parts are located commonly used exterior spaces such as the entrance area, courtyard, "outdoor room", and moon-viewing deck area. A new way of life involving the outdoors was actively encouraged . . .'

House in Nerima
Tokyo, 1986

Above: Exterior view at dusk.

Right: View from living room.

57

Atelier in Tomigaya
Tokyo, 1986

Above: second floor studio.

Left: Exterior view,
showing diagonal extension
resembling a crane.

**Atelier in Tomigaya**
'I was asked to design a building that would have the maximum volume permitted by law on this triangular, corner site, and this determined the exterior form of the building. On the street facade, I added a membrane consisting of a series of solid and perforated aluminium panels cut out in cloud-like patterns over a surface consisting of concrete and glass. I also incorporated something that extends diagonally into the sky and that resembles a crane. In a place like Tokyo where structures are constantly being rebuilt, a crane gives a landscape a feeling of vitality. The crane here is a symbol of that vitality and unfinished quality. The see-through perforated aluminium appears to shift with subtle changes in inside and outside light conditions. To this is added aluminium's quality of reflecting the surrounding landscape and the color of the sky. As interior lights start to go on in the evening, the round window gains prominence . . .'

## Shonandai Cultural Centre
written by Keith Krolak of Itsuko Hasegawa Architectural Design Studio

Fujisawa, a satellite community of Tokyo, is both a residential community and an industrial area, and as such, it is characterized by a considerable flow of people and information. Recently, the city has begun to discard its ties with the existing social structure of Tokyo, opting for a more distinctive, independent culture of its own. The brief called for three main facilities: a municipal hall, a multi-purpose hall, and a children's museum. To be mixed in were restaurants, exhibition spaces, recreation facilities, plazas, etc. Hasegawa's design is a reaction, a pocket of resistance against all that has been excluded by modern planning in postwar Japan. As with all of her previous work, the design originated with the site and the needs of the users as opposed to beginning with a dominant architectural or political theme . . .

Hasegawa believes that many things possible in architecture have been distorted in the name of modernization. Gone are the universal and religious characters of forests, mountains and shrines. The mysterious and symbolic characters that were products of human coexistence with nature, and the maze-like character and neighborhood ambience of Japanese cities have been abandoned in the names of economic growth and progress.

In trying to incorporate into the Shonandai project all that has been excluded by modern planning, Hasegawa discovered that she was designing not so much a work of architecture, but rather a 'topography'. Thus the forms suggest plateaus, rivers, bridges, trellises, forests, mountain ranges, fields, oceans, and the limitless skies. Cosmic elements representing the earth and universe are seen in a pair of giant globes floating above the entire composition.

The building is arranged in two layers; an underground membrane containing a public hall, exhibition spaces, official areas, mechanical rooms, and parking; while the above ground level houses the 'topographical' galleries, workshops, performance areas, etc. The underground peripheral wall organization allows for a structural system devoid of beams. At the same time, the ground level portion is supported from below, permitting a completely independent and lightweight steel structure to occur.

Above: Model of the Shonandai Cultural Center, Kanagawa, 1987–.

# Annabel Jankel *film and video direction*

**Biography**
Born 1955 in Stanmore,
Middlesex, England. Educated
at: West Surrey College of Art
and Design, England, studying
animation, 1973. Worked on
'Ubu Roi', Geoff Dunbar's Arts
Council funded film, Grand Slam
Partnership Ltd, 1976; evenings
spent collaborating with Rocky
Morton on 'Marx For Beginners'.
Joined Rocky Morton's
Cucumber Studios in 1978 and
worked on promotional video for
Elvis Costello's 'Accidents Will
Happen'; collaboration
continued with videos for,
amongst others, the Tom Tom
Club, Rush, Debbie Harry, Chaz
Jankel, Miles Davis, King
Trigger, Donald Fagen, Nick
Heyward. Also worked on title
sequences in 1978 including
those for 'The Tube' and 'Friday
Night videos'; commercials
include those for Quatro, Pirelli,
Wilkinson Sword, Capital Radio
and Fiat. Compiled the book
'Creative Computer Graphics'
with Rocky Morton, 1983.
Commissioned by Channel 4 and
Chrysalis to devise means of
linking pop videos for a series,
1984: with Rocky Morton and
George Stone, 'Max Headroom'
is created; they devised and
directed his debut pilot film,
April 1985. This was followed by
a 13 week series, 'The Max
Headroom Show'. Made the
twelve minute commercial for
General Motors in USA through
Jennie & Co, New York, 1985.
Also made commercials in UK
through Jennie & Co, London,
1986. Closed down Cucumber
Productions as a commercials
production company, 1986;
Cucumber Productions now
developing feature projects;
Directed 'Dead On Arrival' for
Buenvista/Disney in Los
Angeles, 1987. Son Jackson born
in September 1987.

When Annabel Jankel and Rocky Morton first joined forces as animators in 1978 under the title of 'Cucumber Studios', they shared a common frustration with the limitations that then existed in the animation world. They felt it was still entrenched in the 'cartoon' concept of animation that had developed from the forties, but with neither the finance nor the innovation of that period.

Both Jankel and Morton had art college backgrounds and looked for inspiration from the Fine Arts – not from cartoon images – and especially from painters with a strong sense of design. Their main sources were Matisse, Mondrian, Malevich and Miro (all M's) and it was particularly this sense of design that they wanted to emulate in their work.

They also had in common an initial desire to become live action directors. Both had been persuaded to study animation because of their artistic ability and both had, in the process, become 'hooked' on animation. But they found themselves, time and again, looking to the 'real' image, rather than to the cartoon.

Their first project as 'Cucumber Studios' proved to be their first major step towards live action. In 'Accidents Will Happen', a pop promo for Elvis Costello, they found it impossible to realise Costello as a cartoon character, and so took a series of photographs of him with a motordrive and used that as their basis. This started them off in a whole new direction; they increasingly used live action as a basis for their work, and gradually began combining live action and animation. At first the technique was not popular with the advertising agencies, but gradually their unique talents were recognised and their combination technique became Cucumber's hallmark.

During the thriving period of the late 1970s and early 1980s, Jankel and Morton made promos for Tom Tom Club, Rush, Debbie Harry, Chaz Jankel, Miles Davis, King Trigger, Donald Fagan, Nick Heyward and others. They also made a number of popular title sequences for television, such as 'The Tube' and 'Friday Night Videos', and many advertising commercials: Quatro soft drinks, Pirelli, Wilkinson Sword, Capital Radio, Seat cars, etc.

Computer graphics was another area of exploration in the early days of Cucumber; one of the exciting products of their desire to lift computer graphics out of a formal, technical mould was their commercial for Quatro drinks. Dissatisfied with the fact that developments (at that time) in computer graphics were only covered by 'scrappy magazines', they compiled their own book on the subject entitled *Creative Computer Graphics*, published in 1983.

In 1984 they were commissioned by Channel Four and Chrysalis to devise a means of linking pop videos for a series of programmes. Together with George Stone, they created the character 'Max Headroom' and devised his story as an idea for a film to pilot the series. Channel Four agreed and they directed the 'Max Headroom Story' which was broadcast in April 1985, and followed by the 13-week series 'The Max Headroom Show'. Max's story was their first major production and not only took the public by storm . . . but subsequently became an international cult.

They closed down Cucumber Productions as a commercials production company in 1986, and it now exists for the development of feature projects. In 1987 Jankel and Morton directed their first full-length feature film, 'Dead on Arrival', for Buenevista/Disney in Los Angeles.

Also in 1987 (a red letter year) Annabel Jankel gave birth to her son, Jackson.

*Taken from a paper by Kate Symington of Cucumber Productions in London.*

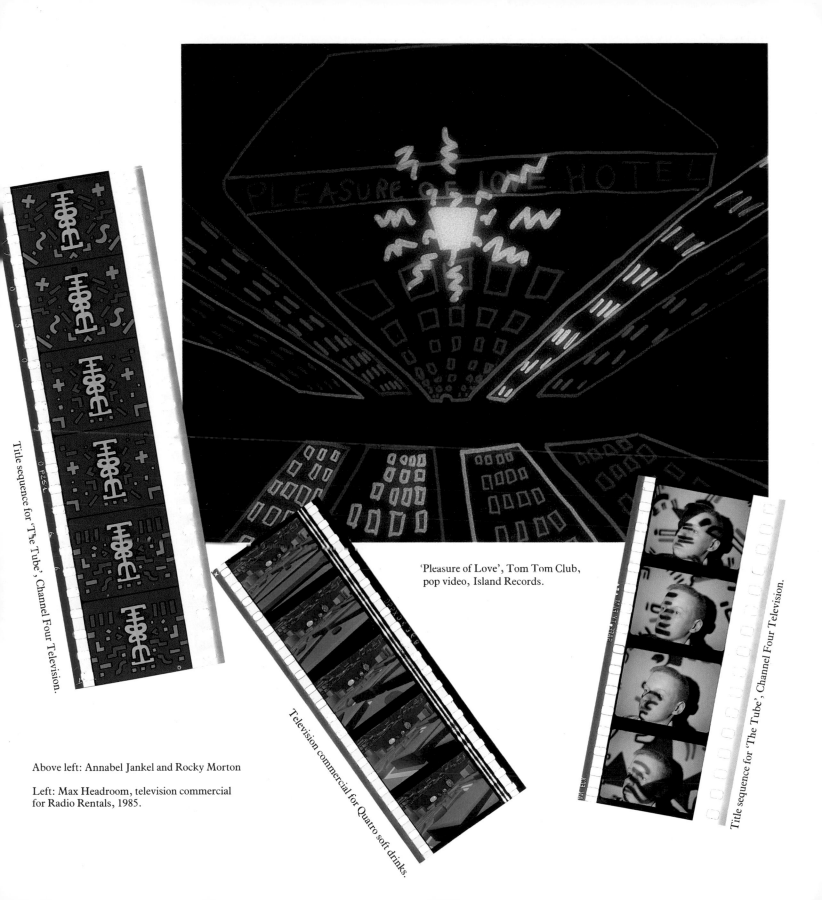

Title sequence for 'The Tube', Channel Four Television.

'Pleasure of Love', Tom Tom Club, pop video, Island Records.

Television commercial for Quatro soft drinks.

Title sequence for 'The Tube', Channel Four Television.

Above left: Annabel Jankel and Rocky Morton

Left: Max Headroom, television commercial for Radio Rentals, 1985.

# Britain

# Eva Jiricna *architecture and interior design*

**Biography**
Born in Prague, Czechoslovakia.
Educated at: the University of
Prague, qualified as an engineer/
architect, 1962; Prague Academy
of Fine Arts, MA, 1963. Arrived
in the UK, 1968, and worked for
a year with the GLC school's
division before becoming an
associate with Louis de Soissons
Partnership, working on the
Brighton Marina project. In
1980, set up her own practice
with David Hodges. Formed
Jiricna Kerr Associates in 1985,
which became Eva Jiricna
Architects in 1987. Selected
works: 1980–82 (with David
Hodges) – Le Caprice restaurant;
Eva Jiricna flat; Joseph Ettedgui
flat 1; Kenzo shop; Joseph
Tricot, Sloane Street. 1982–85 –
Joseph Ettedgui flat 2; L'Express
Café; Pour La Maison, Sloane
Street; Joseph Tricot, Paris;
Lloyds Headquarters interiors
(with Richard Rogers
Partnership). 1985–87 (with
Jiricna Kerr Associates) –
Harrods Way-in department
refurbishment (with future
Systems); Joseph Tricot, Paris;
Joseph Bis, Sloane Street; Pour
La Maison, Draycott Avenue;
Joe's Cafe; Joseph Tricot,
Draycott Avenue; Joseph Pour la
Ville, Brompton Road; Legends
nightclub and restaurant; Vidal
Sassoon Sanctuary; Vidal
Sassoon hair salon, Frankfurt;
Thompson Twins flat
refurbishment and recording
studio. Awards: AD awards for
Eva Jiricna flat, Joseph Ettedgui
flat 1, and Kenzo Shop, 1980–82;
competitions – 3rd Prize,
Robertsons leisure park for
Battersea; 1st Prize, Robertsons
Hampton site in Trafalgar
Square; 1st Prize, GLC
development for Westminster
Pier, with David Hodges; Prize
for innovation, Dunlopillo
competition. Work shown in
numerous diverse publications,
including: *Architectural Review*,
1981–; *House and Garden*, 1979,
1982, 1985, 1987; *Vogue*, 1984;
and *The Face*, 1985.

During the last five years, Eva Jiricna has continued to enjoy a reputation as one of Britain's most influential architects and designers.

Jiricna was born and educated in Prague, qualifying as an engineer/architect. She left Czechoslovakia in 1968, came to London and worked for one year as an architect with the Greater London Council schools' division. She then joined the Louis de Soissons Partnership where she worked for eight years on the planning, design and construction programmes for Brighton marina, and in 1980 formed her own practice with David Hodges. The year 1980 also marked her change in direction – from architectural projects requiring complex technical solutions, to the sophisticated interior design work she is known for today.

In the early 1980s she gained initial recognition through awards she received in a number of architectural competitions, such as the Westminster Pier competition which she won with David Hodges. Further acclaim followed the various commissions she completed for the fashion entrepreneur Joseph Ettedgui, including interior design for a series of his Joseph shops (fashion retail outlets) and Ettedgui's own Knightsbridge apartment.

As time went on she was acknowledged for her revolutionary approach to interior retail design and, faced with a growing number of large retail programmes, formed Jiricna Kerr Associates in 1985 with Kathy Kerr. The team now numbers a total of ten and, under the new name of Eva Jiricna Architects, encompasses architecture, interiors, furniture and component design.

Stemming from a Modernist approach to design, Jiricna's work is renowned for its stylish inventiveness. The use of light and reflection to create illusions of space, ingenious handling of awkward spaces (so common to London's old buildings) and meticulous detailing are all hallmarks of Jiricna's designs. But a most popular feature of her work is the way in which she integrates industrial materials and components into her interiors. Industrial clamps, wiring, tubes etc find their way into home and office alike . . . transformed into 'style', but indicative of her intense interest in function and practicality, and her belief that 'function creates its own aesthetic'.

Shop entrance, Joseph Pour La Ville on Brompton Road, London, c.1985–87.

Balustrade and roof light near entrance of Joseph Pour La Ville on Brompton Road.

Eva Jiricna

'Legends' restaurant and nightclub, 1986.
The brief required a nightclub in the basement and a dining space which could be used during the day and in the early evening. Hence one space light and the other entirely dark. The ground floor ceiling undulates to hide the services. An effort was made to make the spaces appear as large as possible. The staircase, designed as a central unifying feature, sparkles at night.

Above: View of front entrance door on ground floor.

Top: Staircase leading from ground floor to basement (with dance floor).

Left: View of eating alcove from bar on ground floor, showing undulating ceiling.

# Britain

# Natasha Kroll *television and film production design*

**Biography**
Born 1914 in Moscow. Educated at: the Reimann School of Art, Berlin. Teacher of window display at Reimann School of Art, London, 1936–40. Store display manager for Messrs. Rowntree of Scarborough and York, England, 1940–42. Display manager and later Head of Design and Presentation at Simpson Piccadilly Ltd, 1942–55. Joined BBC Television in 1955 as Head of Studio Design Unit, responsible for all talks programmes; Senior Designer, 1956. Drama programmes include sets for 'Lower Depths', 'Death of Danton', 'The Duel', 'Ring Round the Moon', 'La Traviata', and 'The Sponge Room'. Since 1966 freelance TV designer for BBC, Yorkshire Television and London Weekend Television. Productions include: 'The Seagull', 'Family Reunion', 1966; 'Eugene Onegin', 1967; 'The Soldier's Tale', 'La Vida Breve', 'Mary Stuart', 1968; 'Doll's House', 1969; 'Macbeth', 1970; 'Three Sisters', 'Cherry Orchard', 'Rasputin', 'Wild Duck', 1971; 'Hedda Gabler', 1972; 'The Common', 1973; 'Love's Labours Lost', 1975; 'Very Like a Whale', 1982. Film production designer for: 'The Music Lovers', 1969; 'The Hireling', 1972 (FTA Film Award for the Best Art Direction 73); 'Absolution', 1978. Exhibition designs include display work for: Festival of Britain – Lion and Unicorn Pavilion; Finmar Glass and Cutlery Exhibition, 1958; the British section of Milan Triennale, 1964. Publications: *Window Display*, The Studio Publications, London and New York, 1954.

Natasha Kroll was born in Moscow in 1914, and at the age of ten left Russia with her mother to settle in Germany. She was educated in Berlin and came to London in 1936 to teach window display design at the newly opened Reimann School of Art. (Other members of staff at that time included the artists Milner Gray and Pearl Falkiner).

In 1942 she joined Simpsons (Piccadilly) Ltd, one of London's most famous clothing stores, as their display manager. Upon taking over the design of the window displays she recalls, 'the windows became very successful and I had, more or less, *carte blanche*. I could really do what I wanted. A lot was written up about them and people came to look at them.' The Simpsons window displays received international acclaim, and are remembered by many Britons to this day for their wit and imagination. 'It was just that I thought there were no laws about how you present merchandise and what you should do . . . no preconceived ideas, just follow your own judgement and be lighthearted about it.'

Kroll commissioned leading artists such as André François to work on her projects, and was often sent by Simpsons to America and the Continent to attend fashion shows, pick up ideas or 'absorb European culture'. In addition to working at Simpsons, Kroll worked freelance on a number of exhibition displays for the Tea Centre and other organisations, and also designed the Lion and Unicorn Press pavilion for the Festival of Britain.

She had worked with Simpsons for 13 years when one day she was approached by an advertising agency to do a television commercial, freelance. She phoned her friend Richard Levin, Head of Design at the BBC, to ask advice on what fee to charge and was promptly told, 'Don't be silly! Don't go work for them, come and work for the BBC.' Her response was 'Make me an offer.' They did, and she accepted.

So Natasha Kroll joined the BBC in 1955 as Head of the Studio Design Unit. Her brief was to create a new image for talks programmes. This she accomplished by stopping the use of 'those corny little sets' (simulated rooms) and introducing nebulous, atmospheric backgrounds of light and shadow, and graphic effects using photography. The Unit was responsible for all talks programmes, including arts programmes (such as 'Monitor') as well as music and women's programmes. She also tried drama programmes at this time, and gradually

moved away from SDU work to concentrate on 'Play of the Month'. She was considered to be an expert on Russian plays, particularly Chekhov.

In 1966 Kroll was awarded the distinction of Royal Designer for Industry by the Royal Society of Arts for her work in shop display and television design. She also ended her contract with the BBC that year and from 1966 onwards operated as a freelance television designer for the BBC, Yorkshire Television and London Weekend Television, producing literally hundreds of programmes.

In 1969 film director Ken Russell, who had worked with Kroll on the BBC Monitor programmes, asked her to join him as designer for the film 'The Music Lovers'. When explaining the complexity of the job, she can't now recall exactly how many sets she designed for it, except that the number was 'enormous'. Three studios were used to produce interior sets (at least thirty of them), a reconstruction of Moscow was built on the film studio lot, and film was also shot on location. Greenwich (London), for example, doubled as St Petersburg . . . 'and we built a house in The New Forest, for instance. I'd forgotten about that!' 'The Music Lovers' was her first film; she moved on to design five films in all and cites 'The Hireling', directed by Alan Bridges in 1972, as her favourite.

Kroll continued to design both films and a large number of television plays, often undertaking both at the same time. Her last television play was designed as recently as 1982. As to which medium she preferred: 'The quality of films is so much better than television, but it does tie you up for much longer periods of time. You don't see anybody for months on end. You have to write off about four months on a film. But the result is very satisfying.

'Television programmes are more immediate . . . not so *final*. And I like improvising. You can't improvise on films, but you can improvise on television to some extent.'

Above: Natasha Kroll

Left: Window display for Simpsons (Piccadilly) Ltd, 1949.

Right: A humorous prop, from Kroll's book *Window Display*, 1954.

Left and far left: Indoor studio sets for 'The Cherry Orchard' by Anton Chekhov, BBC Television, 1971.

Right and far right: Moscow reconstructed on the studio lot, Ken Russell's film 'The Music Lovers', 1969.

65

# Italy    Mary Little *furniture design*

**Biography**
Born 1958 in Northern Ireland.
Educated at: Ulster Polytechnic,
BA in Furniture Design, 1981;
Royal College of Art, London,
MDes, 1985. Professional
experience: commissioned to
make occasional table from 1981
BA (Hons) Degree Show;
constructed and painted the
'Davis Table' to a design by
Floris van den Broecke for the
book *Master Pieces;* design
assistant for architects Faulkner
Brown Hendy Watkinson
Stonor, working on furniture for
leisure centres; freelance designer
for interior designers Maurice
Broughton Associates, working
on furniture for shops and
restaurants; constructed
armchair from 1985 Degree
Show, Royal College of Art
(batch of armchairs being
constructed and sold by Neotu,
Paris). Began working freelance
in Milan, 1986, for various
studios including Daniela Puppa,
Franco Raggi, Emilio Ambasz,
Nanni Strada, and Massimo
Morozzi. Diverse projects
include bathroom accessories,
wooden chairs, belts, dining
tables and tea-sets, bags for
school children, lamps and sofas.
Lamp designed for Memphis,
launched in November 1978;
currently developing work for
Vitra, a Swiss manufacturing
company. Visiting tutor at
Glasgow School of Art, Scotland,
Loughbrough College of Art &
Design, England, and
Wimbledon School of Art,
England. Work in permanent
collections: 'The Armchair', La
Musée des Arts Décoratifs, Paris.
Exhibitions: 'Experimental
Furniture', Octagon Gallery,
Belfast, Northern Ireland, 1983;
'Young Blood', Barbican,
London, 1983; 'Master Pieces',
Hille Showrooms, London, and
Museum of Modern Art, Oxford,
1983, and at 'Woodworker',
London, 1984; ASB (UK)
Marketing, London, 1985; 'La
Créativité Britannique',
Printemps, Paris, 1985;
'Armchairs', Neotu, Paris, 1985;
Caravelles 'Enjeu de l'objet', La
Musée des Arts Décoratifs,
Lyons, France, 1986.

The unconventional furniture designs of Mary Little
are inspired by ordinary, everyday activities and
needs. Their often curious appearance derives from
serious consideration of function and purpose, and an
acute tuning-in to the human body . . . for the body
and its moods, postures and movements are integral
elements of her designs.

She graduated from the Royal College of Art in
1985 and after a short period of independent work in
London, decided to launch herself professionally in
Milan. By the end of 1986 she had started to work in
Milan on a freelance basis, collaborating with the
studios of Daniela Puppa, Franco Raggi, Emilio
Ambasz and others.

Her aim is to design for production, and to this end
she intends to continue freelancing while establishing
her own industrial contacts. She will be developing
her work with the Swiss manufacturing company,
Vitra, over the next year.

A few notes follow from Mary Little about the way
that she works:

'My interest and work are fundamentally based in
the "domestic domain". I love the home, the house, I
need it. For me it represents the chance to be at my
most relaxed and creative, and to live my own life.

'Traditionally women have been interested in
building and maintaining good homes. I've taken this
way of thinking to extremes, and have found myself
in the profession of looking at the home within a
contemporary context – which means looking at it in
greater depth, and providing for it at a more distant
but perhaps more influential level . . .

'My joy is in studying how furniture can relate to
the human body in its various daily activities,
eg. sitting and having a conversation with a friend,
getting dressed, sitting at a table. I am inclined to
follow a logic – sensibly (re)considering the function
of objects – while at the same time intuitively
working on the "feelings" that a piece will bring
about. The form, the tactile quality, colour
combinations, the simple directness or the richness of
a piece: they all come into this. These seem to me to
be relevant contemporary issues. My current
responsibility is to find companies that appreciate
these values and that fund development of furniture
with this degree of attention.'

Mary Little and a prototype bag inspired by the movement
within a loose, woollen winter coat, 1986.

'A piece that was in response to the growing awareness, of the time, that beauty couldn't be applied and wasn't enough anyway. Instead good health, fitness and regular, all-over, bodycare routines were essential. This furniture has a wooden bench – good for sitting on wet or not dressed – a rubber footpad, exercise bar, storage, worktop, mirror and soft lamp. Castors and pivots give the furniture mobility which is useful when a lot of tasks are being carried out in one space.'
1985

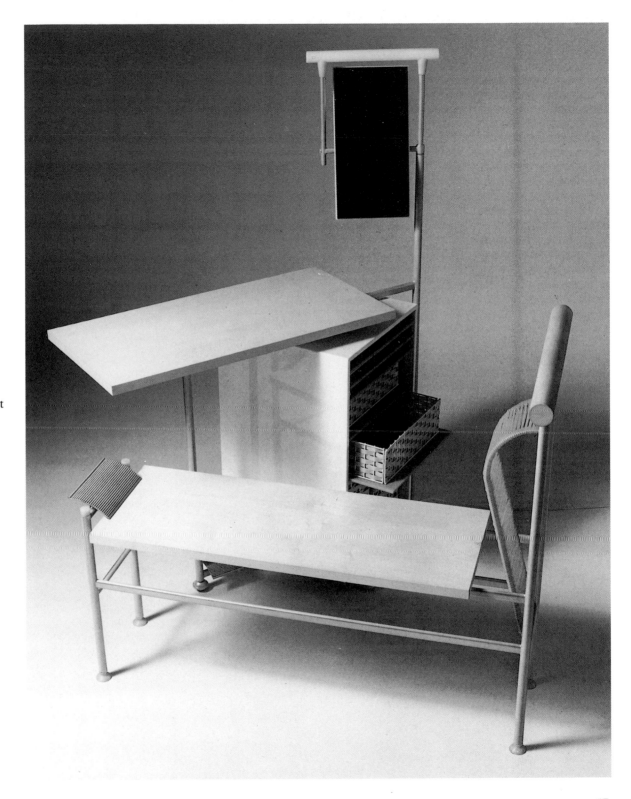

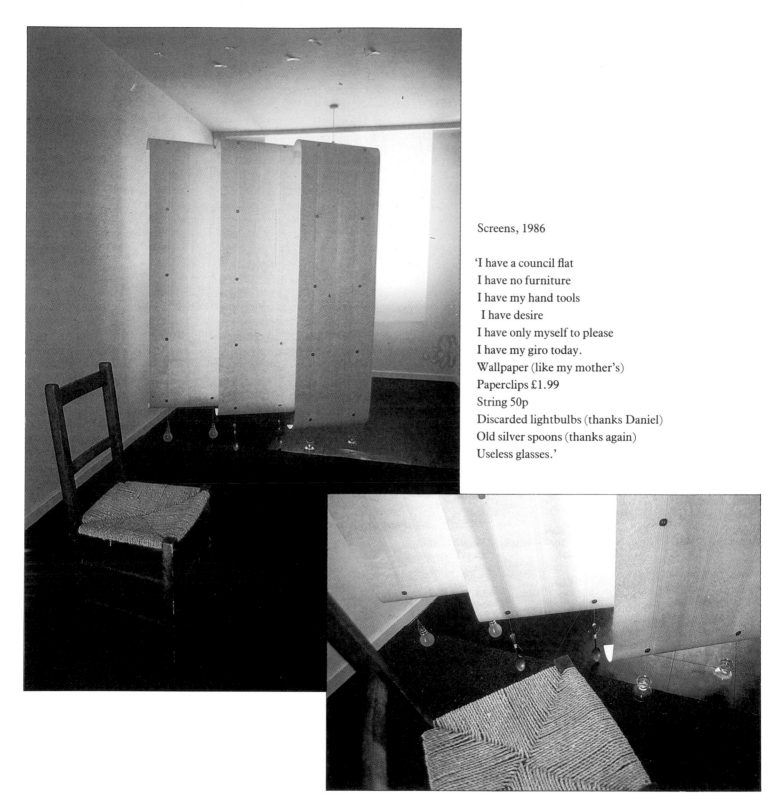

Screens, 1986

'I have a council flat
I have no furniture
I have my hand tools
 I have desire
I have only myself to please
I have my giro today.
Wallpaper (like my mother's)
Paperclips £1.99
String 50p
Discarded lightbulbs (thanks Daniel)
Old silver spoons (thanks again)
Useless glasses.'

'The Armchair' by Mary Little, 1985: 'The chair comes from the
exploration of my experience of sitting in a particular position where I am
at ease in company. I am relaxed and self assured with my arms resting at
different levels, my body is casually supported at one side and my legs are
crossed – always right over left. In company I sit forward and alert when
I am involved in conversation, as I lean back I can relax and listen.
I unconsciously move my body to follow the conversation around the room.
The form of the arms and seat and of the understructure have been in total
response to this. The aesthetic is intuitive with an image that I can identify
with. In this chair I rest assured of my position in the room.'

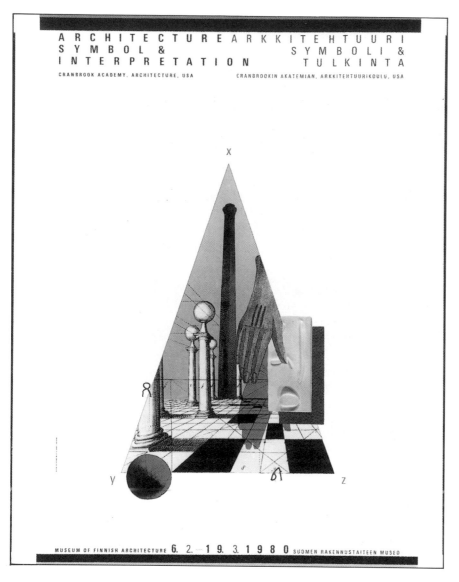

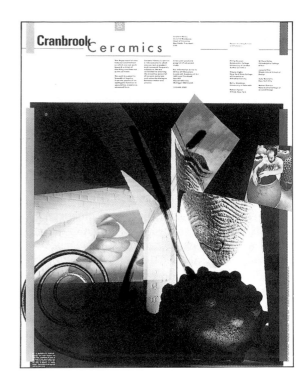

Above: 'Architecture, Symbol & Interpretation' poster (with Daniel Libeskind), Cranbrook Architecture Department, 1980.

Above right: Cranbrook Ceramics poster, Steven Rost photographer, 1987.

Right: Cranbrook Academy of Art poster, Rik Sferra photographer, 1978.

Left: Interior design (with Michael McCoy), Formica Corporation Sterling Executive Office, 1985.

Below: McCoy & McCoy brochure (with Michael McCoy), 1977.

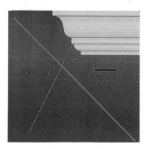

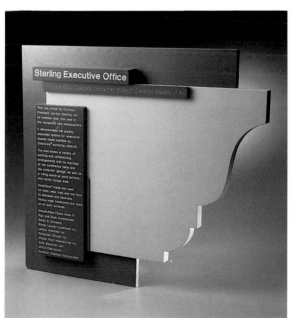

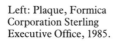

Above: Invitation, Formica Corporation Sterling Executive Office Reception, 1985.

Left: Plaque, Formica Corporation Sterling Executive Office, 1985.

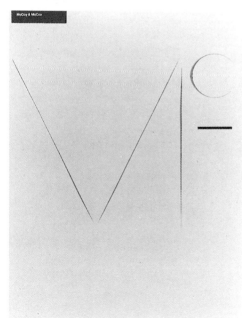

# Britain

# Alison Milner *three-dimensional design*

**Biography**
Born 1958 in Sevenoaks, Kent,
England. Educated at: St Mary's
School of Nursing, trained and
worked as a student nurse, 1978–
81; Middlesex Polytechnic,
England, BA in Three
Dimensional Design (Furniture
Design) 1985; Royal College of
Art, London, MA in Furniture
Design, 1987. Received Princess
of Wales Award for most
distinguished female entrant at
Royal College of Art, 1986.
Currently freelance designer
Projects include: chair made in
conjunction with textile designer
Caroline McKintey, exhibited at
Texprint Trade Fair and in a
Design Council touring
exhibition, 1986–87; the design
of a range of bedroom furniture
for batch production by India
craftsmen for India Works,
Chelsea; and the design of a glass
screen (private commission). Her
'Mirror Lamp' won second prize
in the Design Council
competition 'British Design in
Japan' and was exhibited in
Seibu Department Store,
Tokyo, 1987.

Alison Milner defies classification, and floats freely across a number of three-dimensional disciplines; although her qualifications are in furniture, much of her work has been environmental or sculptural.

She finished her MA studies at the Royal College of Art in the summer of 1987, and shortly after won an award in the Design Council competition 'British Design in Japan' for her Mirror-Lamp entry (*shown here*). About the Mirror-Lamp she writes:

'College was a time to do a lot of research work. I spent one summer holiday analysing the concept of a "stand" as a basic furniture component; most chairs, beds etc are just "people stands". I have constantly referred back to this work and feel the Mirror-Lamp benefited from it. While appearing very sculpturally decorative, the Mirror-Lamp in fact has a form clearly dictated by function; it is the choice of materials and proportions that create its decorative appeal.

'The Mirror-Lamp also illustrates another of my preoccupations: the effect of objects on their surroundings, creating different atmospheres. The idea of using light reflected from a mirror came to me when I was living in an attic room with small skylights and a lot of mirrors.'

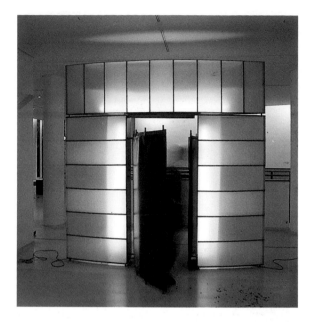

Right: Alison Milner

Above: Doorway, illuminated part constructed from MDF frame and glued plastic 'vellum', entrance part constructed from welded steel tube and pop-riveted Smaragd plastic flooring, 1987.

stacked

cradled

dangled

hung over

inserted

gripped

balanced

propped

Above: Mirror-Lamp, totally adjustable halogen lamp and mirror reflector, made from oak veneer, brass, mirror and glass, height 4ft, 1987.

Left: Eight sketch models of the relationship between stand and object, 1986.

# Marie Neurath *visual communication*

**Biography**
Born 1898 (née Marie
Reidemeister) in Brunswick,
West Germany. Education:
university, studying mathematics
and physics, 1917–24; art school,
1919. Teaching experience,
1922–3. Joined Otto Neurath in
work for the Social and Economic
Museum in Vienna, 1925. Visited
Moscow, as instructor in
transformation, during the
winters of 1931–2 and 1932–3.
Removal to The Hague, 1934.
Visited New York and Mexico,
1936–7. Flight to England with
Otto Neurath, internment, 1940.
Released to Oxford, marriage to
Otto Neurath, 1941. Worked
with Otto Neurath, and a new
team, 1941–5. Otto Neurath
died, 1945. Continuation of work
in Oxford, 1946–8. Moved to
London, 1948. Co-operated in
various serial publications,
several Isotype book series and
filmstrips, 1948–72. Invited to
Nigeria by the Government of the
Western Region, for the
production of visual material for
civic education, 1953. Started
work in 1959 as co-editor of
several volumes of the Vienna
Circle Collection (vol 1, 1973).
Retired from Isotype work, and
the Otto and Marie Neurath
Isotype Collection is established
at the University of Reading,
1971–2. Died 1986, in London.

Marie Neurath

Marie Neurath died in 1986 and from hereon shall remain larger than life. She is described by those who knew her as sensitive, dedicated, courageous, and cheerful despite the turbulent times she lived through. Her achievements lie not only in her long term involvement with 'Isotype', but also in her activities as editor and translator of Otto Neurath's writings, undertaken in her later years. However none of these accomplishments can be truly appreciated through the statement provided below, and readers are encouraged to pursue the various people, events and philosophies surrounding the Isotype Movement through other sources . . . But for the moment, here follows a quick introduction to the Isotype story.

The end of the First World War found Austria in a mess, suffering from food and housing shortages, poor public health, and high inflation. Such alarming conditions provided the background against which Otto Neurath and his team created and developed ISOTYPE (International System of Typographic Picture Language). Isotype, stated briefly, was concerned with the graphic presentation of information – particularly quantified information. It centred on two important principles: the first was the principle of presenting greater quantities by the repetition of symbols (as opposed to proportional enlargement); the second principle was that perspective must not be used, for when the size of equal objects is related to distance from the viewer, quantifying becomes difficult.

Otto Neurath (a social scientist in modern terms) was the creator and key thinker behind Isotype. He became Director of the Gesellschafts- und Wirtschaftsmuseum in Vienna in 1925, and his aim to educate the ordinary people of Vienna, and elsewhere, in the social and economic issues of the time led to the creation of the Isotype team. At this point Marie Reidemeister (later to become Marie Neurath) joined him to work in the museum, and became dedicated to Isotype work for the rest of her life. The efforts of the Isotype team in the Vienna years (1925–34) centred on the making of charts, for publication or display in the museum, showing the linked relationships between housing, health, social administration and education. In short, Isotype was intended to communicate the state of society to people in the street.

Political pressures of the time forced the Isotype operation to leave Vienna and move to The Hague in 1934, and produced a further flight to Britain in 1940. The Isotype Institute was founded in 1942 under the direction of Otto and Marie Neurath (by then married). After Otto Neurath's death in 1945, Marie Neurath took over and directed the work of the Institute for nearly 30 years. During this time she furthered the use of Isotype in new areas, such as in the production of educational books for young readers. After closing the Isotype office in 1972, her last years were centred on the editing and translation of Otto Neurath's writings.

So much for a skeletal overview of Isotype . . . but Marie Neurath's contribution to the Isotype approach requires special attention. Marie Neurath had a central role in the Isotype team: in Isotype language, she was the 'transformer'. The transformer was responsible for taking information or data (collected by economists, historians, and statisticians) and translating it into visual terms so it could be easily understood.

The transformer therefore occupied a crucial place in the design process, and acted as intermediary between the experts (those with specialist knowledge), the graphic artists who actually drew the symbols and executed the artwork, and the public or readers. He or she was a visual editor, so to speak – described in Otto Neurath's words as the 'trustee of the public'. The transformer also bore the responsibility for making clear and interesting statements, but not distorting or exaggerating the material in any way. It is in the role of the transformer that the real art of Isotype lies, and which distinguishes it as an approach concerned with visual judgement and data selection – as opposed to being a stiff set of rules by which boring statistics are automatically turned into boring rows of little men (or women for that matter).

Marie Neurath was the Isotype team's longest working and most experienced transformer, and personified this key element in the Isotype approach. It is convenient to add here that Isotype was essentially a product of teamwork, and when at its height in the 1930s, was produced by the group comprising Otto Neurath as information collector, Marie (Reidemeister) as transformer, and the German artist Gerd Arntz as graphic artist. A model example of their collaboration is the book *Modern*

*Man in the Making* by Otto Neurath, published in 1939 by Alfred A Knopf, New York – a prime opportunity to see Isotype in action.

Thankfully the Isotype story is now well documented and The Otto and Marie Neurath Isotype Collection rests at the University of Reading with people who keep its spirit and attitudes very much alive. Isotype's influence on the work of present day graphic designers has been great: it has passed on the concept of the transformer – an aid to the design of today's complex information systems, providing a necessary bridge between expert and reader. Further to that, Marie and Otto Neurath must be seen as pioneers of visual education, working during a period when words were considered the main learning instrument and pictures didn't really matter. Last of all, and perhaps its greatest attraction: Isotype was a graphic design innovation created in response to the need for social reform and, more broadly speaking, a product of the belief that education is an instrument for social change.

*Postscript*: Much of the information contained here was taken from 'The significance of Isotype', Michael Twyman's introductory essay in the catalogue *Graphic communication through Isotype* (Department of Typography and Graphic Communication, University of Reading, 1975) which was originally published in connection with an exhibition of Isotype work; other information sources were assorted articles by Robin Kinross, particularly 'On the influence of Isotype', *Information Design Journal*, Vol 2 No 2, 1981. All of the visual material related to Marie Neurath was supplied by The Otto and Marie Neurath Isotype Collection at the University of Reading, and thanks are due to Professor Twyman for making it available.

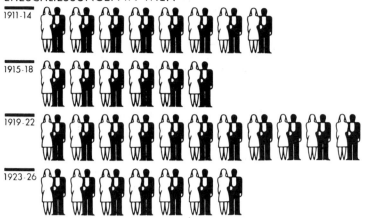

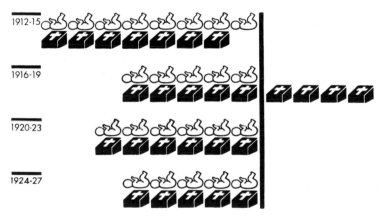

Above: Two charts designed by the Isotype team, from *Bildstatistik nach Wiener Methode in der Schule* by Otto Neurath, Vienna, 1933.

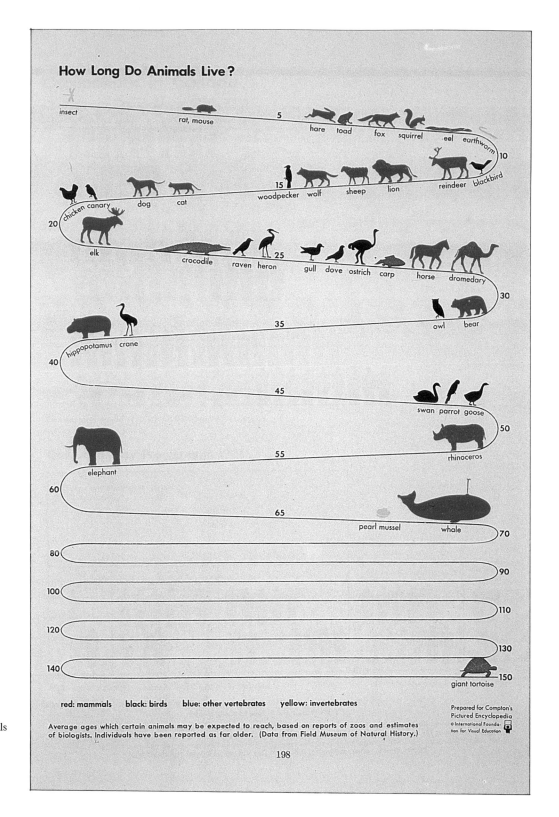

Right: 'How long do animals live?', from *Compton's Pictured Encyclopedia*, Chicago, 1940 edition (appearing on p198 of Volume One.)

Right: Pages from Marie Neurath's notebooks, dated 1941, showing sketches for charts on health education: one (near right) telling the 'Story of Malaria', and the other (far right) providing cautionary advice about the spread of disease.

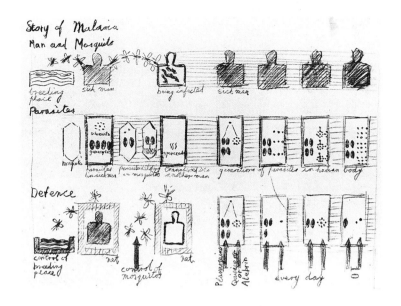

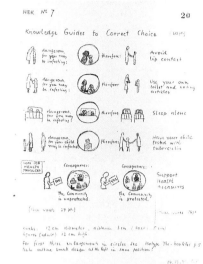

# A BRITISH COUNCIL CHART ON THE NATIONAL HEALTH SERVICE

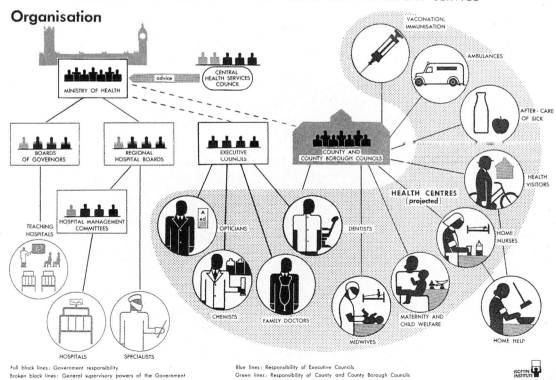

Left: 'A British Council Chart on the National Health Service' showing the organisation of the health service, by the Isotype Institute, 1968.

# Italy

# Nathalie du Pasquier *printed textiles and furniture design*

**Biography**
Born 1957 in France. Finished
school in Bordeaux, 1975; no
further studies. Travelled
between 1975–78. Arrived in
Rome, January 1979; worked as
an au pair. Moved to Milan,
September 1979. Started working
with George Sowden, 1980. First
Memphis collection, fabrics and
decorations for pieces by George
Sowden, 1981. Has since
produced work for all Memphis
collections including textiles,
furniture, carpets, and objects.
Worked for Fiorucci, 1982.
Exhibitions with Sowden on
decoration: a collection of twenty
patterns on paper; a collection of
objects for the home 'Objects for
the Electronic Age'; carpets for
Palmisano 'Ten Modern
Carpets'. Other work: graphics,
textiles, tiles, moquettes,
ceramics, clocks (for Lorenz, and
jointly with George Sowden).
Textile design, mainly for fashion
companies: Pink Dragon,
Missoni Kids, Esprit, NAS
Oleari. Still lives and works in
Milan.

Much of the visual electricity of early Memphis decoration can be attributed to the patterns of Nathalie du Pasquier. Working with George Sowden in the early 1980s, her startling decorations found their way onto textiles, furniture, carpets, objects, and more recently have run riot on fabrics for internationally-known fashion companies (Pink Dragon, Missoni Kids, Esprit and others).

Here follow a few notes by Nathalie du Pasquier – they have not been edited or 'starched' into proper English, for fear of flattening the spontaneity and energy by which they came hurling through the post . . .

'I have had no education in art or design. Probably the travels I did between '75 and '78 made a strong impression on my young mind. Then I learned "doing" design while being close to creative people (George Sowden in particular).

'Not being a specialist of anything I have felt free to absorb a lot of different subjects, but I think I have always remained a bit of a dilettante. I enjoy very much having the ideas and doing the first sketches, then I get lazy for the transformation into a product; it is probably why I am better in designing surfaces, where there is no further work than the first drawing.

'Where do I get my ideas from? I guess from my own brain, they depend on how happy, or sad, or nervous I am. In certain cases they also depend on what my client wants from me. Sometimes I have a theme and try to adapt, but I think I have in my head a catalogue of shapes and rhythms I play with and mix and colour according to what I need.

'Recently, I have also done patterns elaborating drawings I did with the computer; that is very interesting because you don't recognize my hand and you don't know where these images came from.

'I tend to work very quickly, don't do preparation drawings, throw myself on the paper with the colours. Most of the things I do are never sold, they remain in the drawer and often I take them again and

Nathalie du Pasquier

cut them or take some elements and mix them with other things. I like re-doing traditional types of fabrics in my own hand – flowers, paisleys . . .

'Even though I am going on working in the design field, two years ago I started painting and in the last year it has taken most of my time and energy – and is a very different type of concentration and work. At the moment, it is more the direction I want to take.'

Left: Carpet (wool) for 'Palmisano Edizioni Tessili', 1986.

Top of shoe box, for Camper/Spain, 1985.

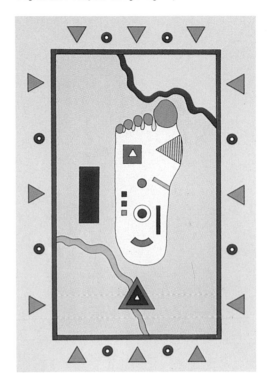

Fabric for Memphis, 1982.

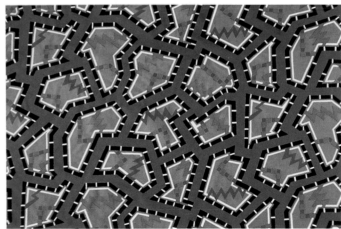

81

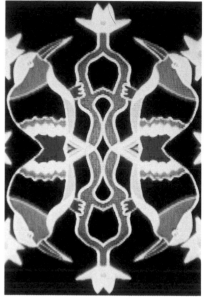

Above: Pattern, using a computer, 1986.

Left: 'Denise' armchair for Memphis, incorporating a fabric using the pattern described above, 1987.

Drawing for a Bathroom, 1985.

# Britain

# Jane Priestman *design management*

**Biography**
Born 1930 in Stevenage,
England. Educated at: Liverpool
College of Art, England. Own
design practice, 1955–75, mainly
working with architects on
interiors, exhibitions, schools.
Joined British Airports Authority
as full time Consulting Designer,
1975; appointed Design
Manager, then General Manager
of Architecture and Design at
BAA, 1978. Appointed Director
of Architecture, Design &
Environment to British Railways,
1986. Fellow of the Chartered
Society of Designers; Honorary
Fellow, Royal Institute of British
Architects; Fellow of Royal
Society of Arts. Member of
Design Committee of the Board
of London Regional Transport;
Member of Design Management
Group of the Chartered Society of
Designers; Chairman of
Environment Panel for BBC
Television Design Awards;
Council Member of Design &
Industries Association; Member
of NEDO Design Working
Party; numerous judging panels
for the Design Council and Royal
Society of Arts & Civic Trust.
Chartered Society of Designers
award for Design Management.

Jane Priestman is recognised as one of Britain's top ranking corporate design managers. She studied at Liverpool College of Art, subsequently worked for both Heal's and Marks & Spencer, and eventually ran her own design group – mainly working with architects on interiors, exhibitions and schools. Then beginning in 1975, she spent ten years managing design for the British Airports Authority (comprising seven airports), and during that time was responsible for part of the modernisation of London's Gatwick and Heathrow airports. The BAA work was an important period for her – one in which she feels 'great leaps' were made – and it was for this work that she received the Chartered Society of Designers Award for Design Management.

In 1986 she was appointed Director of Architecture, Design and Environment for British Rail, reputedly one of the world's most complex and intensive transport networks. It is also, historically, the organisation the British public loves to hate – not only for its long-standing reputation for unreliable service, but also for a visual image of jumbled styles (ranging from historic sites to fast food) and general run-down tattiness.

Priestman took on responsibility for the co-ordination and implementation of a unified corporate design image for British Rail, which takes in every aspect of the railway: from the design of stations and trains, landscaping of railway areas and bridge-painting, to staffing uniforms, cleaning and maintenance, combatance of vandalism, and workforce morale. Lest the scale of the undertaking goes unappreciated, it is worth mentioning that there are 2500 stations involved, 'very big cathedral ones, as well as unmanned leftovers in the middle of nowhere', and 850 listed buildings.

Her approach could be viewed as having two main intentions: one is to introduce a unified look (a corporate whole); the other issue, and just as crucial, is to improve BR's taste by educating everyone, high and low, in the design proposals she establishes. This is being done through the issue of design instruction manuals, and a variety of strategies for boosting the morale of the workforce, and generally building respectability and pride among its members.

Under Priestman's influence, design is now being acknowledged by British Rail as having a key role to play, both in the way that different parts of the organisation relate to each other, and in the way BR relates to its passengers. In her own words, 'With the changing pattern of railway travel we are becoming more aware of the importance of design as an ingredient of passenger service and business success.'

Although the British public may forever mock (as they do with the weather), it is difficult not to notice the improvements taking place over the past year – products of what has to be one of the toughest corporate renewal projects around.

Jane Priestman

84

Jane Priestman's co-ordinated design approach for British Rail involves the bringing together of three major design areas: architecture, design and the environment. New design policies are carried forward by the drawing up of comprehensive design guides, to ensure that consistency of future design and standards of cleanliness, service and style are maintained.

The aim is to have the following areas of design acting in unison so that features complement each other:

*The products* – trains, ticket machines, electronic equipment, special vehicles – mainly the work of design engineers and industrial designers;

*Physical environment* – stations, depots, workshops, car parks, office buildings, ticket offices and travel centres, interiors, shops and toilets – mainly the work of architects, design engineers, interior and landscape designers;

*Information systems* – signs, posters, advertising, timetables, promotional literature – the work of graphic designers and typographers and industrial designers.

Crystal Palace Station: Entrance/Frontage

HST 125: New Intercity Branding

Hull Station: Ticket Office & Travel Centre

Milton Keynes Station Concourse

Richmond Station: Barrier Line

Waterloo Station Concourse

# Italy        Daniela Puppa  *architecture and design*

**Biography**
Born 1947 in Fiume, Veneto,
Italy. Educated at: Milan
Polytechnic, graduating in 1970.
Magazine work: writer and editor
for *Casabella*, 1970–76; chief
editor for the design magazine
*Modo*, 1976–83; currently
consultant for the monthly
fashion design magazine *Donna*.
Her work as an architect has
included: interiors for Driade,
Gianfranco Ferré, Montres and
GFF Duty Free; a showroom for
Fontana Arte in Milan; shops for
Granciclismo (racing bike/sport's
goods) in Milan and Viareggio;
chain of shops for Morassutti/
Metropolis (up-dated their
collection of products
worldwide); currently consultant
for the Croff/Rinascente chain of
shops, on their image and
products. Her work as a designer
has included: fabric collections
for Alchimia and Stucchi
furnishing; a collection of table
objects for Tachikichi (Japanese
Department Stores); a collection
of furnishing fabrics for
Limonta; operative research into
artificial materials and their
possible application as furnishing
fabrics, for Limonta; work for
many other companies such as
Driade, Vistosi, Kartell, Flou,
Carrara and Matta; currently in
collaboration with Fontana Arte,
Cappellini International
Interiors, Sisal Collections,
Tendentse, Irmel and Roset
(France). She also works in
fashion design and since 1979 has
been responsible for the
accessories collection for
Gianfranco Ferré. Has
participated in exhibitions such
as: 'L'Oggettoo Banale', Venice
Biennale, 1980; 'Sezione Design',
15th Milan Triennale, 1981;
'L'oggetto Naturale', Prato,
1982; 'Provokationen design aus
italien', Hannover, 1982; 'Le
case della Triennale', 16th Milan
Triennale, 1984; 'La Neomerce',
for Montedison, Triennale,
1985–Paris, 1986; 'Donne
designers italiane', ADI-
Takashimaia, Tokyo, 1985; and
'Phoenix' Avanguardia of Italian
design, Toronto, 1985. She lives
and works in Milan.

Architect and designer Daniela Puppa has worked internationally in various design fields, as well as collaborating with Italian design magazines as editor and journalist. She was on the editorial staff of *Casabella* (1970–76), then chief editor of *Modo* (1976–83), and at present she is design consultant to the fashion design magazine *Donna*. Puppa has also been the author/creator of influential exhibitions, including (as co-author) 'The Banal Object', part of the Venice Biennale in 1980, and 'The Natural Object' at Prato in 1982.

Her wide-ranging design activities have encompassed products, furniture and fabric collections. She has conducted operative research into artificial materials and their possible application as furnishing fabrics (based on the materials and

technology of the fashion design industry). In the field of fashion design, Daniela Puppa has been responsible for collections of men and women's accessories for Gianfranco Ferré and others. And lastly, as an architect, she has designed showrooms and shop interiors for leading European companies. Here she writes about her design approach . . .

## Objects and materials

'I rarely design an object without having it clear in my mind who will produce it. I am more attracted to and motivated toward designing for concrete situations, and after having, for example, visited a foundry or a textile mill. The intrinsic characteristics of every material, their hidden qualities and restrictions are the elements with which I like to

Above: Collection of furnishing fabrics (cotton jacquard) for Limonta, 1984.

Right and above right: Coffee and tea service (porcelain cup, melamine saucer) for Tachikichi department store, Japan, 1984.

explore new forms and unsuspected uses. Following this vocation free from ideology, I have realized textures with three-dimensional decoration using natural and artificial materials without instituting hierarchies between the two. It doesn't always mean dealing with absolutely new materials, but more often working by "transfer" from the more evolved field of fashion to interior design, and vice versa. In order to structure the different properties and material qualities into usable forms, I like to consider the achievement of a "neutrality" of the objects with respect to time and fashion as a primary objective, without losing the timeliness of the project. I enjoy working on this wavelength, creating precise, neutral forms and soft-spoken decor that do not exalt themselves at first sight, but rather unfold gradually.'

Left: Daniela Puppa

Left: 'Newport' bench system for Cappellini International Interiors, 1984. The system of legs allows the transformation from table to bench.

87

# Italy

# Barbara Radice *art and design direction and writing*

**Biography**
Born in Como, Italy. Educated
at: Catholic University of Milan,
graduated in Modern Literature.
Associate editor of *Data*, a
contemporary art magazine
published in Milan, 1974–76.
Began working as a freelance
journalist, 1977, writing for
magazines, such as: *Modo,
Domus, Casa Vogue, Japan SD,
Wet, Art & Auction*. Since 1981
has been consultant art director
for Memphis, in charge of
exhibitions and cultural
activities. Selected publications:
*Elogio del Banale*, Studio Forma,
Alchymia, 1980; *Memphis, the
New International Style*, Electa,
1981; *Memphis*, Rizzoli, New
York, 1983; *Jewelry by Architects*,
Rizzoli, New York, 1987; *Ettore
Sottsass' Design Metaphors*, Idea
Books & Rizzoli, 1987 (edited
and introduced).

Barbara Radice is the art director, and a founder-member, of Memphis – the international group of architects and designers based in Italy and led by Ettore Sottsass. Radice is not a designer . . . but she performs a critical role as literary and media spokesperson for Memphis, projecting their ideas and activities to an international audience.

To put it another way, she is the PR expert for the group – responsible for handling the media, and in charge of their exhibitions and cultural activities. Working in association with Sottsass, she also acts as a driving force within the group in terms of co-ordination, discussion, and generally 'making it all happen'.

Radice's background is in journalism. She graduated in literature at the University of Milan. From 1974 to 1976 she was associate editor of *Data*, a contemporary art magazine published in Milan. From 1977 onwards she worked as a freelance journalist, writing for *Modo, Domus, Casa Vogue, Japan S D, Wet, Art & Auction* and other magazines, specializing in reports and interviews on architecture, design and the visual arts in general. She became art director for Memphis in 1981.

Radice's book on Memphis (bearing the same title and published in 1983) is a vital collection of the work, ideas, personalities and experiences of that group – essential, and moreover, exciting reading. Other main publications by Radice include *In Praise of the Banal* 1980; *Jewelry by Architects* 1987; and Ettore Sottsass' *Design Metaphors* 1987, which she edited and introduced.

Right: Barbara Radice

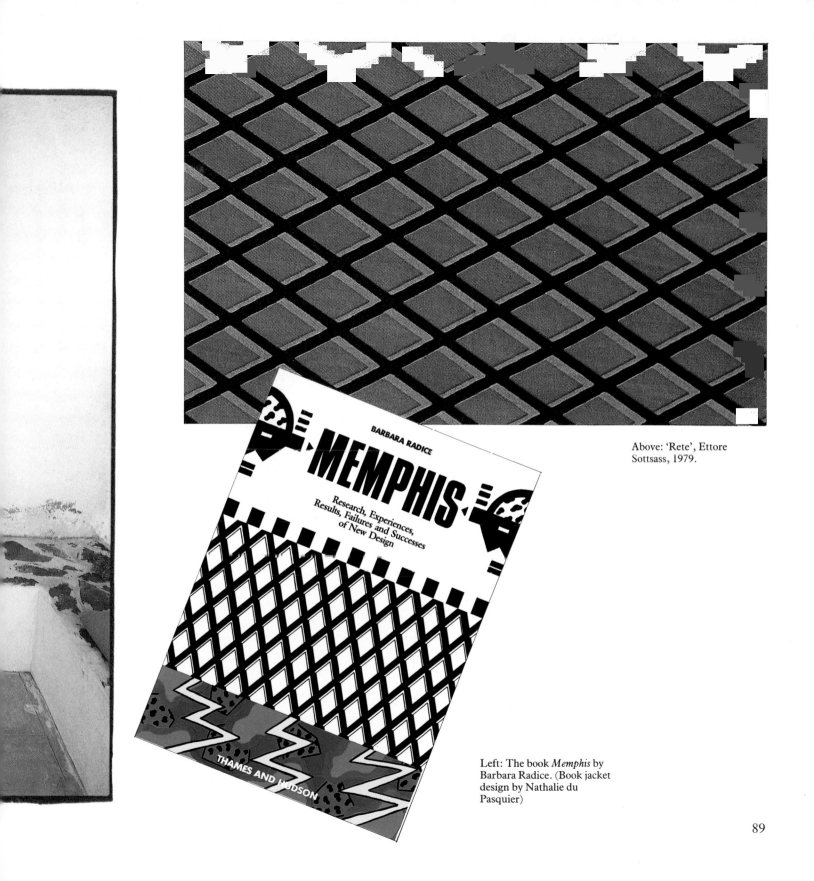

Above: 'Rete', Ettore
Sottsass, 1979.

Left: The book *Memphis* by
Barbara Radice. (Book jacket
design by Nathalie du
Pasquier)

89

# Italy     Patrizia Ranzo *architecture and design*

**Biography**
Born 1953 in Naples, Italy.
Education: Naples, graduated
with a degree in Architecture, in
1981. Has worked in design since
1975. The majority of her design
and architectural work is done in
cooperation with Sergio Cappelli.
Participation in exhibitions: 'The
city as a theatre', with A Branzi,
A Rossi, L Thermes, F Purini,
B Gravagnuolo, and Sergio
Cappelli, at the Napoli Centro
Zen, 1981; Paris Biennale, 1982;
'Unforseen consequences: art,
fashion, design', Prato, Firenze,
1983; 'South wave', Bari, 1985;
'The wonder wardrobe',
Milanovendemoda, Milan Fair,
1986; 'New trends in design: the
neonaturalism', 1986; SEIBU
exhibition, Tokyo and Osaka,
1986. The 'Agave' table,
designed with Sergio Cappelli
and produced by Stildomus, was
selected for the 1987 Compasso
d'Oro exhibition in Milan.
Personal exhibitions: 'The
naturalist's home', with Sergio
Cappelli, Centro Ellisse, Naples,
1985; Jannone Gallery in Milan,
with Sergio Cappelli, 1986. One
of the winners of the 'Women in
Design International
competition' on two occasions;
for Industrial Design in 1981,
and for Interior Design and
Architecture in 1983. Awarded
First Prize for Italian Design,
with Sergio Cappelli, at the
SEIBU exhibition in Tokyo and
Osaka, 1986. Architectural plans
(selected for the Paris Biennale)
published in the catalogue, 'La
modernité ou l'esprit du temps',
1982. Publications: contributor,
*Achitettura e tecnologia
appropriata*, edited by F Angeli,
Milan, 1985; co-author with V
Gangemi, *Il governo del progetto*,
Parma ed., Bologna, 1986; 'The
Mediterranean sensitivity as a
cultural perspective', Chicago
University, Illinois, 1986.

Thirty-three year old Patrizia Ranzo started working in the design field in 1975. She acquired a Degree in Architecture (at Naples) in 1981 and since 1983 has been collaborating on projects with the Department of Configuration and Implementation of Architecture at the University of Naples. She is also involved in research into planning, and has written many papers on the subject.

The greater part of her design and architectural work is done in co-operation with architect Sergio Cappelli. They have an office together in Naples and she describes their working relationship as being very special in design terms . . . 'We work in a symbiotic relationship, rather than as a couple, being united by common tastes and cultural choices.'

Since 1981 Patrizia Ranzo has participated in many exhibitions both in Italy and abroad, and has received many awards. In the Women in Design International competition in California she won an award for industrial design in 1981, and for interior

design and architecture in 1983. Most recently: she won (with Sergio Cappelli) the First Prize for Italian Design in the SEIBU exhibition, Tokyo, 1986; and the 'Agave' table, designed with Sergio Cappelli, was selected for the 1987 'Compasso d'Oro' exhibition in Milan.

The project that she regards as her most important to date is 'The Naturalist's Home', a collection of objects and interiors inspired by the theme of Mediterranean culture. The collection was devised and designed in 1985 with Sergio Cappelli and represents the first stage in a line of research which she hopes to continue in the future. A few notes follow from Patrizia Ranzo on 'The Naturalist's Home':

'The title of my last collection, "The Naturalist's Home", makes reference to an exhibition held in Milan in October '86.

I have to say straightaway that "The Naturalist's

Home" is neither the ecologist's nor the naturalist's home. It is rather the house of a collector of shapes and images bearing a strong Mediterranean characterization.

The exhibition was, in fact, the first attempt to work out a design inspired by the expressivity of the Mediterranean cultural setting.

The ensemble of collection pieces (a table, a chaise-longue, some shelves and some trophy-like mirrors) suggests the image of a home interior where the natural world and fragments of Mediterranean culture change into the matter and subject of design.

The pursuit of a new figurativeness is the thread running through the choice of materials (volcanic stone, marble and tufa for tables, steel and inlaid wood for shelves). It is closely connected with the idea of a new figurativeness which is no longer abstract, and is fully inherent in the industrial language, being more deeply rooted in the idea of place, culture, expressivity.

Mediterranean culture as a culture of differences and a culture basically rich in expressive values is the aspect that we want to bring to light.

The Mediterranean has never been a homogeneous area, neither from a cultural viewpoint (being a patchwork of highly diversified peoples and cultures) nor from a geographical. Consequently, the expression of its material culture amounts to an aggregation of differences, having in common the identification of an ideal, theoretical, everyday life pattern – an expression of one's own cultural identity which, through a very strong force, is projected onto material objects.

I believe that this identification in objects is a fundamental theme that must be resumed, after the levelling down effected by industrial culture in the language of objects. Thanks to this element, Mediterranean culture has become a theoretical model that can be imitated beyond geographical and cultural borders.'

Patrizia Ranzo and Sergio Cappelli

a Ferrante Imperato, naturalista napoletano del XVI secolo

'The Naturalist's Home'

Right: 'Agave' table

Left: 'Agave' table, steel structure and gray volcanic stone or white marble plane, prod. Stildomus/Italy. The container for plants can be removed and replaced by a fruit bowl, chopping-board, or a candlestick.

The Naturalist's Home Collection:
'Trophy-like shelves' made
of inlaid wood and steel, 1985.

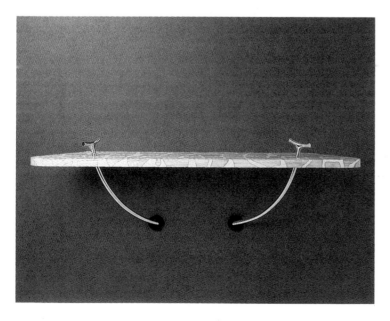

Project for a temporary theatre,
Naples 1981, with Sergio Cappelli
and Andrea Branzi.

# Britain

## Sarah Reed *audio visual design and production*

**Biography**
Born 1949 in Kent, England. Educated at: Canterbury College of Art, 1965–6; Ravensbourne College of Art, 1966–7; Hornsey College of Art, 1967–70. Work experience: freelance designer, 1970–2; Texprint 72, Design Centre, 1972; Buyer at Biba, 1972–3; freelance AV designer/producer, 1973–8; founded and ran Edco Reed, production unit making multi-image programmes, 1978–84; sabbatical in USA, 1984; Edco Reed sold to Saatchi Group, 1985–6; Director and Head of Multi-image Triangle Two, 1986–. Visiting Lecturer at: Ravensbourne College of Art, 1971–2; Hornsey College of Art, 1971–2; Preston Polytechnic, 1982–3; Bournemouth and Poole College of Art, 1986–. Visiting Professor at the Royal College of Art, 1985–6. External Assessor at London College of Printing, 1986–. Exhibitions: Boat Show, Earl's Court, 1973; Museum of Geological Sciences, 1974; World Wildlife Fund 20th Anniversary, 1979; Launch of The World Conservation Strategy, 1980; World's Fair, Knoxville, Tennessee, 1982; National Museum, Singapore, 1983; 25th Anniversary World Wildlife Fund, 1984; Three Architects, Royal Academy of Arts, 1986; The Enterprising Scot, Royal Museum of Scotland, Edinburgh Festival, 1986. Television work: programme trailers for Central Television; commercials – Philips Philishave and Saft Mazda. Chairman of Judges, Images Festival, 1984–7; Chairman of BISFA Multi-image Group, 1984–6, 1988. Awards: Images Festival Awards – four Gold, two Silver, two Bronze; Images Patsy Award, (awarded for contribution to audio visual industry), 1986; American Association of Multi-Image Silver Award, 1987.

Over the past decade Sarah Reed has been involved in the design, direction and production of audio visual and video programmes for major festivals, museums and corporations (internationally). In 1978 she founded Edco Reed, a production unit making multi-image programmes, which she ran until 1984. In the two years that followed, Poppy and Alexander Reed were born, and since 1986 Sarah Reed has been Director and Head of Multi-image at Triangle Two production house in London. Her statement follows . . .

94

Left: Stills taken from an audio visual programme produced for Kodak entitled 'Remembering is Feeling'; photography by Richard Dudley Smith. Captions are taken from the poem 'The Truly Great' by Sir Stephen Spender, on which the programme is based.

(top)
*Touched with Fire*
Photographic collage composite using background photograph of wall texture, overlayed with contrasting texture, on fine grain release positive, abstract sections of distressed type characters O C H, title, and black and white portrait of Tuscan farmer, soft edged into background.

(centre)
*The Morning Simple Light*
Photograph of hot springs, overlayed with farmhouse, wall texture, distressed type characters N G and title.

(bottom)
Black and white portrait of Tuscan farmer with his dog, superimposed on distressed photograph of logs and scythes.

*Film stocks included*:
Tri-X, EPR 135–36, Kodalith 2556 Type 3, Ektachrome Dupe Film 5071, Ektachrome EPY 404 5018, Fine Grain Release Positive 5302.

'I trained vaguely as a textile designer; I wasted most of my first two years at Hornsey College of Art. I couldn't quite work out why I had been accepted on to such a good course in the first place with students who were obviously so much more talented; nor what I was then supposed to be doing.

It was during a ten-week summer trip to America, travelling around 7,000 miles in an old beetle that I began to understand what I might be able to do. I always think of the image of Frankenstein's monster being given life by his creator as the closest example of my own personal penny dropping.

I returned to my third year of college inspired, re-energised, and ravenous; pulled off a reasonable body of work, confounded the sceptics, and escaped into the real world relatively unscathed.

Co-incidentally and almost by chance, I put together an audio visual programme for the degree show. An utterly primitive affair consisting of my photographs from the American trip with some sort of music track, unsynchronised. A crude attempt, but nevertheless for me it was an important, if not significant career statement.

America has been ever since, a great source of inspiration, catalyst to ideas and general life energiser. All visits are major therapy for me, feeding an insatiable hunger for ideas, and visual images.

After the almost inevitable post-college period of uncertainty and confusion, in 1973 I worked on my first major multi-image programme, an ambitious project creatively and technically. I threw myself into the medium with all the energy and naivety of an enthusiastic amateur. I had no experience of sound design other than learning piano as a child, but the whole complicated and laborious task of assembling the individual elements of the programme was (and still remains) endlessly fascinating.

On reflection, for me to use the screen as a medium of expression was fairly obvious. I found a language in which I could communicate, despite all my inadequacies: a language employing the use of design, pictures, music and words, all enmeshed and integrated into a single unified message with the elements drawn together into a kind of generic screen-speak. But a message that could, almost despite its quite extraordinary clarity, be invested with powerful nuances: ambiguity, humour, pathos, irony.

My original training in textile design has served me well, quite by fluke: designing in repeat, framing images precisely, colour awareness, having an eye to fashion, attention to detail, and so on. In its wider context the textile industry has always promoted women, so early on I got a taste for equality.

Any small successes have been gratifying but basically unimportant – consequences of a widening experience and professionalism. It is the work itself that generally provides the satisfaction for me.

If I do any good work, capture something in a programme, it is of no importance to anyone except that I find it interesting *myself*, so then I live with these captured "things" quite comfortably.

But I continue to declare my subjective view: in spite of the fact that many other screen designers are more clever, creative and talented, I must go on making programmes, driven on by an unbounding curiosity, which is never satisfied and continuously renewed. This is the basis for all my artistic endeavours to date and undoubtedly for the foreseeable future.'

Sarah Reed with Poppy and Alex, March 1987.

# Holland

# Monique Renault *animation*

**Biography**
Born 1939 in Rennes, Brittany, France.
Filmography:
1972: 'Psychoderche'.
1974: 'A la Votre'.
1975: 'Swiss Graffiti'.
1978: 'Salut Marie', co-prod. AAA/Nico Crama.
1979–80: Sequences for NOS TV.
1979: 'The Sexual Revolution', prod. Roos Molleman.
1980: 'In Nomine Domini', prod. Roos Molleman.
1981: 'Borderline', prod. Peter Brouwer.
1983: 'OUT!', prod. Roos Molleman.
1984: 'Hands Off', prod. Roos Molleman.
1987: 'All Men Are Created Equal', first of four films, for the animated series 'Blind Justice', prod. Orly Bat Carmel for Channel 4.
1988: 'Pas A Deux', co-real. Gerrit V Dijk, prod. Cilia V Dijk.
Monique Renault's films have received international critical acclaim. All are handled by feminist distribution companies such as 'Cinemien' in Amsterdam, and 'Circles' in London.

*Author's note:* Working as an independent film-maker in Holland, Monique Renault uses the medium of animation to make social and political statements from a feminist stance. Her films are renowned for their comedy and humour; moreover, she takes on issues that many would fear to touch: the Church's historical endorsement of the repression of women, historical rendition and its male bias, women working in a male working world . . . and more recently, the critical subject of wife battering. Her films are shown regularly at festivals in Europe, and are used for discussion in action groups, as well as being shown in cinemas and on television. When I asked her to contribute to this book, she wrote me a letter which I have reproduced here in its original form (with her kind permission). Ignoring the obvious language difficulties, I felt that her story – and its warmth and laughter – ought to be shared.

Monique Renault

AMSTERDAM, 27th october 87.

Dear Liz,

As child, I was never really considered to be able to do anything ... Wel, I liked very much of course not to have to dress the table for dinner or do the washing, for instance, but (ather, the consequences are that it's petty hard to believe in yourself! I am born 25th of october 1939 in Rennes - Brittany - France, as yongest child of 7. With quite a difference in age between them and me. My mother was very conventionnel, very catholic and also very funny. With me, she was completely different than with my 4 older sisters. They had to get married as soon as possible. I did not. I was able to study art. First in Rennes and then in Paris (Ecole Nationale des Beaux-Arts) in 1962. I studied painting. Always with the idea of one day working in animated films. that was the only one thing I was sure about. And also not to get married and not to get any children, before ... long time! they were enough in our family! I was not at all involved in feminism. For about 10 years I have been looking around me, a buite stupid and passive, I think! I was very much interested into men. only their opinions were valable. Only "they" were interesting.

Women ? Pouah. Concurrence ! After 68, like every other people, I started to look at it differently. that was also my first experience with an animated film festival in ANNECY. I got very upset to see the way my colleagues were depainting women. I thought it was very unfair! And I decided to do the same, but reverse. Still refusing to join or to be accointed with any feminist movement. Still devoted to men !

I started my first animated film - "PSYCHODERCHE". A very short story (1 MN.) of a woman ~~kissing~~ a man's bottom and laughing. My male friends were extremely shoked and adviced me not to show a film so bad for my reputation. I was not able to make ~~film~~. I had to stay a good disciplined assistent! I said "thank you... I did not mean to hurt ..."
But oh Ironie, without me knowing it, Marco Ferreri choosed the film to be shown ~~before~~ "la grande bouffe" All France saw it. I started to think differently... Then one day, I meet Nicole LISE BERHEIM. She Had founded with other women ~~cineastes~~ cineastes. "MUSIDORA". Then I realised I was not alone any more. I did not need to be sorry, and feminists were not those terrible amazones... And yes I was a feminist. And I was still beautifull ~~and~~ and did not turn into a bad imitation of a male figure... Together we organised the First Women film festival in Paris in 73, I think. IT was a beautifull time. I started a new film "A LA VOTRE". Working over day in a studio (A.A.A.) as head animator, and making my film during the week-ends. And then

Frame 19:
'Ot En Hoe Zit Het Nou Met Sien?', prod. NOS Television, 1981.

Frame 20:
'Ot En Hoe Zit Hel Nou Met Sien?', prod. NOS Television, 1978.

Frame 21:
Drawing published in *Sextant*, 1981.

Frame 22:
'A La Votre', animated film, prod. Contrechamp, 1973.

97

another one with JACQUELINE VEUVE "SWISS GRAFFITI." ⑤
A film I like personaly very much. Then with my
feminist lugage I came to Amsterdam to work for a
few month. It's now 12 years ~~ago~~ later ... I have
made a child, some more films... I have been working
~~France~~ for Dutch T.V. (NOS.), making animated sequences
for a discussional feminist program. I got mommy
~~f~~rom the government not only to make my own films
but also to make one about the battered wifes,
HANDS OFF. Last year, channel 4 - LONDON - gave us the
mommy to make a film about Women and the law -
called "BLIND JUSTICE." Honnestly, I do not think I would
have had all those opportunities if I had stayed in France.
It's a bite sad to say... But it's so. I like very much
to be in Amsterdam. What I do find difficult is to
educate my boy & as a feminist mother... A question
of love I guess, and I do love him. I often have the
feeling my mother, my dear mother, took her revanche
~~trough~~ me, she wanted me to be different from my
sisters, to have more chance to accomplish myself
than she had. I thank her. AMEN!
♀♀♀♀♀♀♀♀♀♀♀♀♀♀♀♀ ♀♀♀♀♀♀♀♀♀♀♀♀♀♀♀♀♀♀
        Hope to see you in Holland. lot of
Succes. thank you.
                Monique.

Frame 23:
'A La Votre', animated film,
prod. Contrechamp, 1973.

Frame 24:
Sketches for 'Mon Ventre
Est Amoi', 1978.

Frames 25–30:
Cells and background,
'All Men Are Created Equal',
prod. Smooth Cloud, for
Channel Four Television.

# Britain    Su Rogers *architecture*

**Biography**
Born 1939 in Cornwall, England.
Educated at: London School of
Economics, BSc in Sociology,
1961; Yale School of
Architecture, 1961–63.
Professional experience: Partner,
Team 4 Architects, 1963–67,
(won The Financial Times
Award for Reliance Control
Factory at Swindon); Partner,
Richard and Su Rogers,
Architects, 1967–70,
(represented British Architects at
the Paris Biennale, and won
RIBA award for house in
Cornwall); Partner, Piano and
Rogers, Architects, 1970–72,
(winners of International
Competition for Centre
Beaubourg/Centre Pompidou in
Paris); Unit Master,
Architectural Association School
of Architecture, London, and
private practice, 1972–76; Tutor,
Royal College of Art, School of
Environmental Design and
Architecture, 1975–85; Director,
Royal College of Art Project
Office, 1979–86; Partner,
Colquhoun Miller and Partners
Architects, 1986–. Visiting tutor
at: Cambridge University
Department of Architecture;
University College of Wales,
Cardiff; Columbia University,
New York; Bristol University
School of Architecture; Bath
University School of
Architecture; University College,
Dublin; Toronto University,
Canada. External Assessor at:
Manchester Polytechnic School
of Interior Design; Kingston
Polytechnic School of Interior
Design; Plymouth Polytechnic
School of Architecture. Has three
sons and two stepdaughters.

Su Rogers, presently a partner in the London architectural firm of Colquhoun, Miller + Partners, initially trained as a sociologist and planner . . . 'My parental background was very liberal, left wing and concerned with art and design. My first degree in sociology was not enjoyable, and I immediately switched (after obtaining the degree from the London School of Economics in 1961) to studying architecture and town planning at Yale. I have *no* formal qualification as an architect!'

She married architect Richard Rogers and worked as an apprentice with him (which she still maintains is a fine way to learn). They formed Team 4 Architects, working with Norman and Wendy Foster from 1963 to 1967, and continued their partnership as Richard + Su Rogers Architects from 1967 to 1970 (their marriage ended in 1969 but they kept working together) and as Piano + Rogers Architects from 1970 to 1972. It was at this point that they won the international competition for the design of the Pompidou Centre, an exciting experience and a building which Rogers admires but she still considers it an experiment in structures inappropriate for the heart of Paris.

She then left the practice to teach for five years at the Architectural Association, while still maintaining a private practice, and moved on to teach at the Royal College of Art. In 1979 she took over as Director of the RCA Project Office and, among other projects, was responsible for the design of the Henry Moore Gallery, a purpose-built exhibition space intended as a showcase for RCA work.

She left the RCA in 1986 to go into private practice with her second husband, architect John Miller, with Colquhoun, Miller + Partners. One of their current projects is the design of a building extension to house the RCA departments of Graphic Design, Painting, Photography and Film – an adventurous conversion job involving three listed buildings and wildly varying departmental requirements – and this project is considered very significant within the partnership.

Left: Su Rogers

Other current projects include The Nomura Gallery (Works on paper and associated smaller galleries) for London's Tate Gallery, local authority housing, an extension to the Fitzwilliam Museum and a New Town in Spain.

With regard to her personal life, she notes: 'Normally chaotic family life throughout my career, bringing up three sons and two step-daughters. Have never had nannies nor live-in helps, because I believe the only way to establish close contact with your children is to look after them. None the less they all went to nursery school at rather a young age.'

And design issues?

'I am essentially still a "Modernist", but see that the most important aspect of modern architecture is that new buildings, or bits of buildings, whilst being modern in their own right, respect the order and form of the existing city structure. A new building may borrow from the language of the adjoining buildings, but need not ape them.

'For instance, the new concert hall stage which I designed for the beautiful church of St John, Smith Square is an entirely modern piece of design, but subservient to the powerful interior of the church.'

On the subject of women in the field, she is concerned that too few women study architecture and feels that architecture should be suggested as a career option for women in more schools. (Often it is not. For example, when her daughters were at grammar school, career advisers never mentioned architecture.) Rogers also makes it clear that although she recognises the drawbacks for women, she doesn't think feminists are dealing with them in the right way. But she admits that she cannot think of a better alternative. She is definitely against positive discrimination and when women at Cornell University in America invited her to apply for a teaching post because there were no women on the staff she thought the suggestion very negative . . . 'I don't want to be asked because I'm a woman, but because I'm a good architect or teacher.'

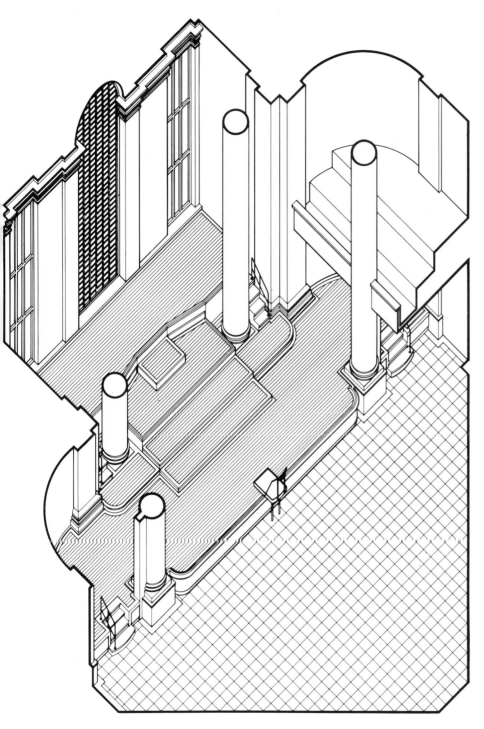

Above: Interior of the Rector's Lodge, Royal College of Art, London, 1980

Above: Axonometric view showing the new stage at the church of St John, Smith Square, London, 1980.

Right: New stage at St John's, Smith Square, 1980.

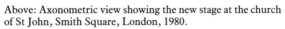

**The Courtyard Building (Henry Moore Gallery), Royal College of Art**

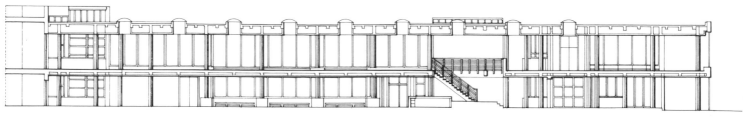

Above: Long section, Courtyard Building

Above: Henry Moore Gallery, view from Lower Level Seminar Rooms, 1986.

Above: Henry Moore Gallery, view of Main Space looking towards Main Entrance, 1986.

**The Courtyard Building, Royal College of Art**
London, 1986

Architects: RCA Project Office
(Su Rogers, Avtar Lotay, Terry Robson, and Norman Chang)
Client: Royal College of Art (Rector, Jocelyn Stevens)

'The Courtyard Building is an extension at lower ground and upper ground floors to the existing Darwin Building. The building extends into the original courtyard and out to Jay Mews where it provides a new front entrance at lower ground level. The three mature plane trees have been freshly landscaped. The upper level accommodates 1000 sq m of temporary exhibition space, known as the Henry Moore Gallery. The lower level accommodates a series of seminar rooms and secondary exhibition space.

'The introduction of an entrance "drum" or circular lobby rotates the visitor onto the main public circulation route which ascends an open flight of stairs and terminates on the upper ground level at the main entrance.

'The Henry Moore Gallery is a multi functional space acting as concourse, exhibition space and the venue for special occasions, seating 500 visitors for the Convocation lunch. It is a light, open space allowing views from Hyde Park through to the Library and Common Room block. Removable floor to ceiling exhibition screens were specially designed to increase the hanging area as required.'

Below: Plan of Level 2 – Henry Moore Gallery,
Courtyard Building, Royal College of Art.
(Level 1 – Lower Galleries and Seminar Rooms
not shown.)

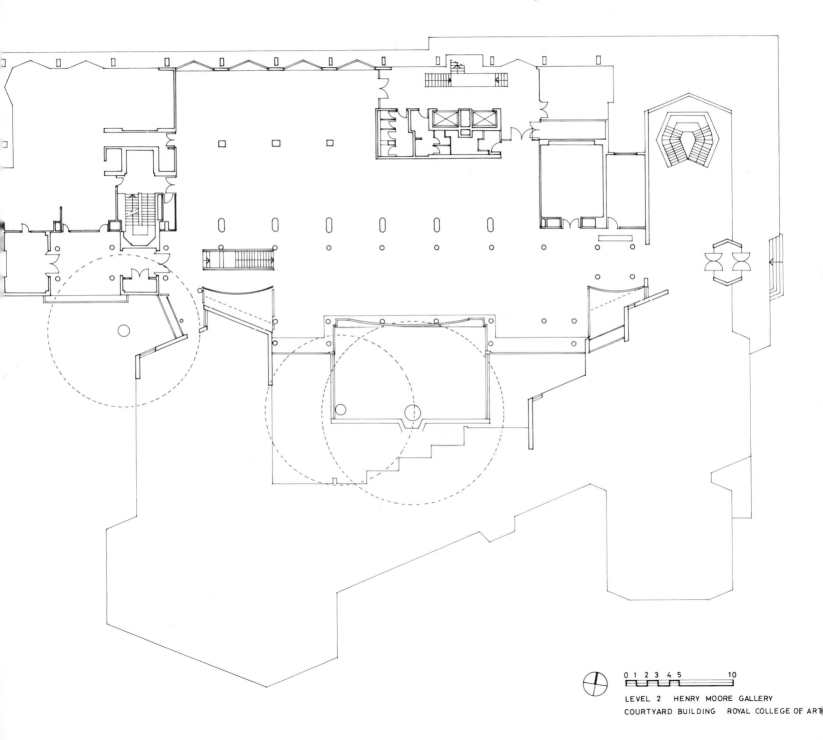

0 1 2 3 4 5          10

LEVEL 2   HENRY MOORE GALLERY
COURTYARD BUILDING   ROYAL COLLEGE OF ART

# Holland

# Marte Röling *graphic design and fine art*

**Biography**
Born 1939 in Laran, NH, Holland. Educated at: Academy of Fine Arts, Amsterdam, 1956–62. Her work is commissioned by art collectors, private companies, and the Dutch government. Work includes: huge sculptures and monumental works of art; postage stamps (for the Dutch PTT); record sleeves (for Philips/Fontana); video; film; posters; theatre sets and costumes; projections; fashion drawings; lithographs and silkscreens. Her official portrait of HM Queen Beatrix of The Netherlands won international acclaim. She uses a diversity of materials in her work, such as plastics, concrete, photographs, wood, paint, metal and glass. Since 1959 she has exhibited work in England, Europe and the USA, and has had more than one hundred one-woman exhibitions, and many group-exhibitions; co-exhibitors have included Picasso, Keinholz, Lichtenstein, and Warhol. She is a member of the Alliance Graphique Internationale. She has appeared on many television and radio shows, and had a starring role in the film 'Herendubbel'.

Marte Röling is, without a shade of doubt, one of Holland's most dynamic personalities – well known for her vibrant character ('kind of crazy' to use her own phrase); her extraordinary, if not baffling, range of activities, as described in the press statement shown here; those *huge* sculptures (yes, they really are that big); and perhaps most important of all, her never-ending attempts to inject life and *fun* into the conservative Dutch establishment . . .

Far right (centre): Press publicity sheet for Marte Röling.

Right: Sculpture entitled 'Wimpel', polyester and glass fibre and high gloss lacquer, approx. 49 metres long, World Trade Centre, Amsterdam, 1985.

104

MARTE RÖLING studied drawing and painting at the State Academy of Fine Arts in Amsterdam from 1956-1962.One of her teachers there was her father professor G.V.A.Röling.Since 1959,when she was nineteen years of age,she started a series of about 125 one-man- and many group-exhibitions in museums and galleries in Europe,England and the USA.Her co-exhibitors were amongst others Picasso,Kienholz, Lichtenstein,Warhol.Apart from dutch schools using her work as a finals-project,much has been written about her and her work in international artreviews,artbooks and the public press.Many television and radio-shows have made MR one of the most wellknown people in Holland.She has a wide range of activities such as making huge sculptures and monumental works of art,with commissions for government buildings, private companies and art collectors,using such different materials as plastics,concrete,photographs, wood,paints,metal and glass.Her official portrait of H.M.Queen Beatrix of The Netherlands won national acclaim.Designing record sleeves (Philips/Fontana),video,film,posters,poststamps for the dutch PTT, theatre sets and costumes,projections,fashion drawings,lithographs and silkscreens and playing a star part in the movie 'Herendubbel' are amongst MARTE RÖLING's many accomplishments.She is a member of AGI. Apart from all that she is recognized as one of the great beauties of her times.

HWPartners production 1984

Left: Marte Röling before her flight in a Royal Dutch Airforce F16, 1987.

Below: 'Polka-dot' tram, City of Amsterdam, 1975.

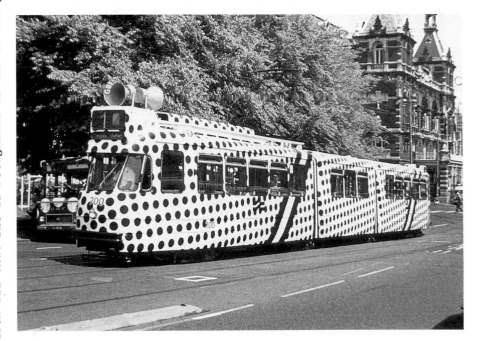

105

# India          # Nina Sabnani *animation*

**Biography**
Born 1956. Educated at: MS
University Baroda, BA Fine
Arts, 1979; National Institute of
Design, Ahmedabad, Certificate
in animation, 1982. Part-time
teacher in a Nursery school,
Baroda, 1979; Part-time assistant
to Potter Daroz, Baroda, 1979;
Teaching assistant, National
Institute of Design, Ahmedabad,
1983–4; member of faculty of
Visual Communication
(Animation), National Institute
of Design, 1985–. Held an
animation workshop for graphic
designers from Indian TV
stations in 1984, and for students
at the National Institute of
Design in 1985. Selected the
Indian films to be screened at the
Bristol animation festival, 1987.
Filmography: 'Drawing!
Drawing!', (3 minutes), black
and white, 1982; 'Energy from
the Atom', (3 minutes), colour,
1983; 'Shubh Vivah', (5
minutes), colour, 1984; 'The
Barter', (2 minutes), colour,
1984; 'Gujari', (2 minutes),
colour, 1984; 'Din Pratidin',
(2 minutes), colour, 1985;
'A Summer Story', (5 minutes),
black and white, 1987. Best
animation film prize for
'Drawing! Drawing!' at the
shorts festival in Calcutta, 1985.
'Energy from the Atom': made
for the Trade Fair Authority of
India, and screened at an
exhibition 'Energy is Life', 1983–
84. 'Shubh Vivah': screened at
Cambridge Animation festival,
England, 1985; telecast by
Channel Four, England, 1985;
distributed in England by
Circles. 'Gujari': screened at
Cambridge Animation festival,
England, 1985; telecast by
Channel Four, England, 1986.
'Din Pratidin': made for the
Directorate of Adult Education,
India; telecast by national
network TV regularly. She
received a two months UNDP
fellowship to travel and study
animation in Belgium, Holland
and England, in 1987.

Nina Sabnani is a 31 year old animator, working professionally and teaching at the National Institute of Design in Ahmedabad, India. Her films have been broadcast by national network television in India, and are becoming increasingly familiar to British animation festivals and television.

In her film 'Shubh Vivah', screened at the Cambridge Animation Festival in 1985, she makes use of the political potential of animation to launch an attack on the dowry system (illegal, but still widespread in India); the film has now become a subject for discussion groups campaigning to end the system. She writes about the making of the film . . . and other things . . .

### About my work
'As a student I thought of animation as a vehicle for wit, directed mainly at juveniles – dignified, of course, by the animator's technical virtuosity. Fortunately, fate intervened in the form of Roger Noake (at the time a UNDP consultant, seconded to the National Institute of Design) who provoked us all into actually thinking about the possibilities of the medium, instead of assuming that they were given – wrapped and packaged – courtesy Walt Disney.

In a country where dramatic contrasts stare you in the face it isn't hard to find content for making films. What is hard is finding a form that is not a kind of ex-colonial mimicry. I don't find it necessary to forge one distinctive style; I think each film demands its own idiom. Since there are so many wildly disparate things I want to make films about, I need, not one appropriate form, but many. I have on two occasions borrowed styles of representation from painters in India. One was for "Shubh Vivah" (Happy Wedding), an anti-dowry film. The drawing style is that of the women painters from Mithila, Bihar and their paintings are ritualistic. My last film, "A Summer Story", used the story and drawing style of Professor K G Subramanyam who, unlike the Mithila women, is a formally-trained painter.

### About myself
I began life as a painter with a degree in fine arts, until an acute teacher declared that my talent was for animation. It was strange being credited with an aptitude for a craft I wasn't sure I could spell, but at the same time I had heard all those stories about lives being changed by sudden revelations. So I gave animation a go and here I am, one more character in those miraculous stories.

I studied animation for two and a half years at the National Institute of Design, Ahmedabad. Ishu Patel of the National Film Board of Canada inspired us every now and then with his films and persuaded the Institute to take some of us onto the faculty. It's a hard job and there's lots to do, but it's been fun.

### An aside: animation and dreaming
Once I realized that animation and dreaming are analogous, I wondered why it had taken me so long to arrive at this conclusion. We respond to both in the same way. We know that they're both "unreal" and yet we suspend disbelief. Within them time shrinks, stretches or even stops. People can be within two places at the same time, or even dead and alive all at once. Quite often a dream character or an animated figure will look like one person and behave like another. Animation is a domain where we can magic the improbable, the absurd and the utterly impossible into existence. If the "real" world is to be put into perspective, someone has to dream.

### An encounter
In 1984, I worked on a film "Shubh Vivah" on the issue of dowry with a few women painters from Mithila, Bihar. Painting for these women is an essential part of their social existence. Their stylized, ritual paintings are made around mythological themes and they paint them at festivals, weddings and other similar occasions.

As a radical departure from the normal function of such paintings, a few of these women had made paintings on the issue of dowry. As victims or observers they were revolting against a socially-accepted norm with a language close to them. I saw these paintings at an exhibition and felt an immediate involvement with their attempt. I suggested to them that we work on an animated film using their drawing style in tandem with my experience as an animator. They were bewildered by the idea of animation, but very enthusiastic nonetheless about the project. What I found most interesting was the appropriateness of the form for such a theme. Usually paintings such as theirs are made to form a part of the preliminary instalment of dowry that seals the marriage contract. And here they are used to frame a polemic against this very system.'

Above: Nina Sabnani

Stills from 'Shubh Vivah' (Happy Wedding)

The film 'Shubh Vivah' confronts the issue of dowry (still widespread in India), and is based on the ritual paintings made by the women of Mithila, Bihar.

Images from Nina Sabnani's film 'A Summer Story'

109

# Britain

# Gaby Schreiber *industrial and interior design*

On meeting Gaby Schreiber, leading British industrial and interior designer, conversation inevitably takes off at a lively pace about work: hers, yours, other people's – and all with equal enthusiasm and interest. She thrives on it . . . and still projects the qualities of sophistication and professionalism that made the press refer to her as a 'tycoon' in her heyday. ('Although *human*, I hope' . . . she adds.) For Gaby Schreiber headed a small empire in the 1960s comprised of three companies: Gaby Schreiber and Associates, design firm; Convel Ltd, a trading company; and Convel Design International, a European design company based in Brussels. But she began to build her empire in the late 1940s when 'design was an exclusively male field'. On this subject she admits that as the field was dominated by men 'it was necessary to work doubly hard to impress with your efficiency'. So it was strong-willed perfectionism and high standards that often saw her chosen over men, and made her successful, despite the heavy competition.

She was born in Austria, and studied art and stage and interior design in Vienna, Florence, Berlin and Paris. She arrived in Britain just before the war, and designed for the plastics industry during wartime. After the war she continued designing in plastic, producing kitchen and catering equipment, tableware, cutlery and a host of other products for cafeterias and chain stores such as Marks & Spencer, as well as designing plastics for building structures and components. Interestingly, although her 'plastics phase' has received a great deal of exposure recently and some of the domestic products earned a place in the Museum of Modern Art in New York, she does not consider it her most important work and clearly favours the large interior design consultancy work that was to follow later in the 1950s.

It was also in the late forties that she set up her design office, 'based on versatility, not specialism'. She built up a team of specialists from different fields – interior designers, product designers, engineers, architects, graphic designers – and formed an organisation handling 'total design projects' or, as she describes it, 'the design of everything from a small teacup to a large building'.

From the 1950s onward, Gaby Schreiber and her team tackled large design projects all over the world, and were responsible for the interiors of aircraft (the BOAC fleet, 1957–63), ocean liners (Cunarder and QE2), department stores, office blocks, hospitals, factories, cinemas, cabin cruisers, restaurants, and conference halls, plus domestic interiors and conversions. Schreiber herself sat on many design juries and committees, both national and international, and her work has appeared in international books and journals on design.

She is still working and is currently concentrating on the collation and publication of her projects and work, while also producing the memoirs of a life full of worldwide travel, glamour and high society, and the hard work of heading an international concern at the top of her profession.

Gaby Schreiber

Right: Unbreakable plastic glasses.

Far right: Melamine stacking cups.

Below: Cabin interior of Boeing 707.

**Interior design scheme for BOAC (British Overseas Airways Corporation)**
Gaby Schreiber and Associates

A perfect example of the Gaby Schreiber concept of a 'total design project' was the interior design of the entire BOAC fleet of aircraft. Carried out from 1957 to 1963, the design scheme incorporated Comets, Boeings, and VC10s, and general updating of the existing fleet.
(The interiors were so impressive that her firm was subsequently commissioned to design the interiors of the Queen's Flight.) The firm was responsible for designing everything inside the aircraft – not just the decor – and started with the interior structure of the aeroplane when it was just a shell and wiring. They undertook the shaping of the interior walls and bulkheads, ventilation grills, lighting, air conditioning and luggage racks; the seating with adjustable tables and headrests; and all the decoration and fittings, from the colour of the cushions to plastic tableware.

Above left: VC10, windows and ventilation grills.

Above right: VC10, emergency escape windows.

Right: A typical specification chart, showing materials to be used for the interior decor (with samples attached). The charts were an innovation created by Gaby Schreiber and Associates to facilitate communication between the many different people/departments working on a complex design scheme.

| SCHEDULE OF FINISHING MATERIALS | LAVATORY FWD STARB'D | REVISIONS | DATE | CLIENT: | DESIGNER: |
|---|---|---|---|---|---|
| TYPE OF PLANE **VC-10**  JOB No. **COL. 101** | **A STRUCTURE 1** | THIS CHART SUPERSEDES ALL ISSUES BEFORE | 20.10.60 | BRITISH OVERSEAS AIRWAYS CORPORATION | GABY SCHREIBER & ASSOCIATES 7, HOBART PLACE, LONDON, S.W.1. TEL. SLO-6127 |

| LOCATION | ITEM | | MATERIAL | COLOUR | WEIGHT | SUPPLIER | REMARKS | COLOUR | MATERIAL |
|---|---|---|---|---|---|---|---|---|---|
| Ceiling | Lining | 1 | PVC cloth 'Raindrop' | Silver grey | 10 oz. or 8oz. per sq. yd. | Deraide Ltd. | | | ALL MANUFACTURER'S SAMPLES TO BE SUBMITTED TO G.S.A. BEFORE PLACING FINAL ORDERS |
| | Roof light | 2 | Reeded perspex | Opal white | | | | | |
| Sidewall (outboard) | Lining above shelf | 1 | PVC cloth 'Raindrop' | Silver grey | | Deraide Ltd. | | | |
| | Light cove | 2 | Stove enamelled alum alloy | White matt finish | | | | | |
| | Side shelf | 3 | Formica | Lavender blue matt 21765 | | De La Rue | | | |
| | Lining below shelf | 4 | PVC cloth suede finish | White | | Wellington Weston Ltd. or ICI | | | |
| | Skirting | 5 | Amtico care-free Vinyl VH12N or VH44N | Harvest white or Harvest Taupe | | Rumasco Ltd | Final decision subject to meeting on 26.10.60 | | |
| | Window reveal | 6 | Darvic plastic | Silver Grey | | I.C.I. | This should match PVC cloth 'Raindrop' exactly | | |
| Bulkhead stn. 191 | Lining | 1 | Panflex 100 series 101-10 | Dull gold | | Polyplaster | | | |
| | Skirting | 2 | Amtico care-free Vinyl VH12N or VH44N | Harvest white or Harvest Taupe | | Rumasco Ltd | Final decision subject to meeting on 26.10.60 | | |
| | Handgrip | 3 | Aluminium alloy anodise | Gold | | | Final colour sample submitted for and approved by G.S.A. on 29.8.60 | | |
| Bulkhead stn. 234.5 | Lining | 1 | PVC cloth suede finish | White | | | | | |
| | Mirror trim | 2 | Anodised alum alloy | Gold | | | | | |
| | Cabinet above counter | 3 | PVC cloth suede finish | White | | Wellington Weston or I.C.I. | See BOAC general notes on cleaning of materials | | |
| Longitudinal bulkhead stn. 191-stn. 234.5 | Lining | 1 | PVC cloth 'Raindrop' | Silver grey | | Deraide Ltd. | | | |
| | Door Lining | 2 | PVC cloth suede finish | White | | Wellington Weston or ICI | See BOAC general notes on cleaning of materials | | |
| | Door Trim | 3 | Anodised alloy | Gold | | | | | |
| | Door Furniture | 4 | Anodised alum alloy | Gold | | | | | |
| | Skirting | 5 | | | | | same material as used on floor | | |
| Floor | Covering | 1 | Amtico care-free Vinyl VH12N or VH44N | Harvest white or Harvest Taupe | | Rumasco Ltd. | Final decision subject to meeting on 26.10.60 | | |
| | | 2 | | | | | | | |
| | | | | | | | | | |

112

Far left: Boeing 707, forward entrance vestibule.

Left: Boeing 707, bar service area.

Left: Perspective view of cabin and seating.

113

# USA    Alison Sky  *architecture as art*

**Biography**
Multi-disciplinary background of
sculpture, poetry, critical writing
and philosophy. Project Designer
and Partner-in-charge of SITE.
Work with SITE, for Willi Wear
Ltd, includes: Women's
Showroom, New York, 1982;
Boutique, Harrod's Department
Store, New York, 1982;
Executive Offices, New York,
1983; Men's Showroom, New
York, 1984. Competition
winning entries with SITE
include: Pershing Square,
Cultural Park, Los Angeles,
1986; Ansel Adams Museum and
Center of Photography, Carmel,
California, 1985; 'Highway 86',
World's Fair Transportation
Pavilion and Plaza, Expo 86,
Vancouver, Canada, 1985. Other
recent work with SITE includes:
Paz Building, Adaptive Reuse
Commercial and Office Complex,
Brooklyn, NY, 1984; Inside
Outside Showroom, Catalog
Showroom, (Best Products Co,
Inc), Milwaukee, Wisconsin,
1984; New York Brickwork
Design Center, New York, 1984;
The Museum of the Borough of
Brooklyn (museum, support
space, and executive offices),
Brooklyn, NY, 1985; Laurie
Mallet House, private residence,
New York, 1985; Theater For
The New City, Center for the
Performing Arts, New York,
1986. Founded the ON SITE
series of publications. These
include the internationally
acclaimed book *Unbuilt America*,
which she co-authored with
Michelle Stone. Fellow of The
American Academy in Rome.
Continues to publish, lecture,
and participate in major
symposiums.

Alison Sky, James Wines and Michelle Stone are
principals of the New York design firm SITE, which
stands for 'Sculpture In The Environment'.

SITE describes itself as an 'architecture and
environmental arts organisation chartered in New
York City in 1970 for the purpose of exploring new
concepts for building and public spaces'. SITE is
committed to reaching beyond architecture's formal
conventions and historical base (ie. architecture as
design) to create architecture as art – an art which
relates to its surroundings, and which communicates
and has meaning for the people who live with it.
Their approach is called 'narrative architecture',
which basically means that buildings and spaces can
reach out to people more effectively if they tell a
story. Their concepts usually evolve out of already
existing physical and psychological information
within a particular context. This attention to 'site
orientation' has allowed them to integrate art,
buildings and context, while still meeting all
functional and economic requirements.

SITE initially brought modern architecture to the
American public's attention with their showrooms
for Best Products Co. Inc. Constructed throughout
the 1970s and scattered around suburban USA, each
highly individual building sported a bizarre facade –
one seemed to be collapsing into a pile of bricks;
another was fragmented into oddly-shaped segments.
They created a dramatic impression of modern-day
decay, and the series became an established feature of
American popular imagery.

In the eighties SITE's diverse projects have
included 'Highway 86' World's Fair transportation
pavilion at Vancouver's Expo 86; showrooms,
boutiques and executive offices for Willi Wear; park
spaces; museums; office complexes and private
homes. SITE's projects and ideas have been
published and reviewed internationally.

Alison Sky has been instrumental in the conceptual
development of all of SITE's work. As Project
Designer, and Partner in Charge, Sky organises,
directs and analyses all project research. She is
involved in the conceptual design of projects from
inception, and remains actively involved in all stages
through to completion. In addition, Sky founded the
*ON SITE* series of books on environmental arts and
architecture, including the internationally acclaimed
book *Unbuilt America*, which she co-authored with
Michelle Stone.

Alison Sky of SITE (Sculpture In The Environment)

**Laurie Mallet House**
New York City, NY, 1985
Architects: SITE Projects Inc

'The Mallet residence is designed for a professional woman and her family in the Greenwich Village area of New York City. The project called for the renovation and expansion of an 1820's, three-story, Greek Revival house in a historic landmark community. The dwelling was originally developed as early speculative housing. Because of neglect, economic construction methods to begin with, and general deterioration, the structure required major architectural work . . .
'The concept for the interior of this house is based on a layering of narrative ideas drawn from its history, context, and the personal biography of its owner. This information was converted into a series of architectural and furniture artifacts which partially emerged from the walls, like ghosted memories that have been invaded by the later additions of several generations of inhabitants. This choice of artifacts is determined by the scale and purpose of each room, and the existing architecture. Most of the objects are consistent with 1820's lifestyle, although a few (like the entrance hall's equestrian references) are based on the owner's personal history.
'This work of narrative architecture is completed only by the addition of a final layer of residential artifacts provided by the Mallet family. The result is that every inch of the interior and garden is invested with historical and psychological cross-referencing.'

Right: Foyer, Laurie Mallet House

# Britain    Alison Smithson *architecture, urbanism*

**Biography**
Born 1928 in Sheffield, England.
Higher Education: University of
Durham at Newcastle-upon-Tyne,
School of Architecture, 1944–49.
Married Peter Smithson,
architect, in 1949. Commenced
work for Schools Section, London
County Council, 1949. In practice
with Peter Smithson in London
since 1950. Best known built work
of partnership: Hunstanton
Secondary Modern School,
Norfolk, (won in competition)
1950–54; private houses;
Economist Building, St. James's
Street, London, 1960–64; Robin
Hood Gardens, Tower Hamlets,
1963–73; Garden Building, St.
Hilda's, Oxford, 1967–69;
buildings at University of Bath,
1980s. Best known projects of
partnership: Coventry Cathedral,
1951; Sheffield University, 1957;
Infant School, Wokingham, 1958;
Churchill College, 1959; British
Embassy, Brasilia, 1964; Lucas H.
Q., 1973; Maryhill Housing,
Glasgow, 1984. Other work:
graphics, 1952 –; furniture, 1953
–; artifacts; clothes (including
shirts for P.S.); exhibitions, such
as: The House of the Future,
1956; This is Tomorrow, 1956;
Milan-Triennale, 1968; Venice
Biennale, 1976; on Christmas,
1978, 1979, 1980. Best known
urban studies of partnership:
studies of cluster patterns,
patterns of association, 1952–58;
Hauptstadt Berlin, 1957–58;
Mehringplatz, Berlin, 1962; Old
City, Kuwait, 1968–70; Damascus
Gate, Jerusalem, 1979;
Lutzowstrasse, Berlin, 1980; Parc
de La Villette, Paris, 1982.
Publications of Alison Smithson:
*Young Girl*, Chatto & Windus
1966; *Euston Arch*, Thames and
Hudson 1968; *Team 10 Primer*
(ed.), Architectural Design 1962,
Studio Vista 1968, MIT Press
1975; *Team 10 at Royaumont*,
Architectural Design 1975; *Tram
Rats*, Arts Net 1976; *Team 10 out
of CIAM*, Architectural
Association papers, 1982; *AS in
DS: An Eye on the Road*, Delft
University Press 1983; *Upper
Lawn, Solar Pavilion, Folly*,
Technical University Press,
Barcelona, 1986. Numerous essays
published internationally since
1951. Teaching: Visiting
Professorships, seminars, studios,
workshops, in Europe and abroad.

Alison Smithson speaks for herself:

'If you work with someone twenty-four hours a day
for forty years, the activity cannot be pulled apart
although in the work our separate "hands" and minds
are obvious.

'Our activity has been on a tangential track to things
happening around us . . . from the beginning our
manner of practice served our concentration on the
search for "what to build towards". Everything we did
was focussed on following our intuition, our instinct
towards developing a language of architecture/
urbanism appropriate to our period; one that did not
"rip off" either the heroic period of the Modern
Movement or the still close 1930s that both belonged
to a life gone by. To feed necessary invention and
rethinking, our activities advanced on a broad front:
ideograms/diagrams; graphics, such as Christmas
cards, page layouts; artifacts; furniture; photography
and writings that we might classify as documentary,

inventive, projective . . .architecture/urbanism.

'We believed the home to be the regenerator of the
energy for life; through our concern for its form and
its grouping, those we met at CIAM 9, 1953 – who
immediately formed Team 10 – drew our orientation
away from London to Europe.

'Neither of us had previously worked in private
practice so our studio is moulded to our life pattern.
As a student I had to commute for five years and in
London circumstances conspired that we began and
continued to live and work in the same place,
enabling a three period working day. It has been our
choice to only build one building at once and the
commissioning pattern has followed this . . . in the
1950s, buildings of all sizes; the late 1950s, through
the 1960s into the 1970s, urban studies; the 1970s
and 1980s, medium sized buildings.

'In the 1980s, we travel more often separately; less
for study; more to take part in activities . . .

and so it goes on . . .'

Alison Smithson at TECTA, Lauenförde opening of Wewerka
pavilion, 1985.

Above: *Landscape* – Triangle Workshop, New York State,
USA, 1987. Sheet plywood 'tree-screen' to signal building's
entrance by extending corner of building out into landscape.

Far left: *Objects* – Celebratory Gear, Flags 1965. Bride's Blossom: pink flowers on white drogue, white cut-out flowers on pink drogue.

Left: *Built work under construction* – Folly, Upper Lawn, near Fonthill. Under construction: modified box-frame, detail. Photographed 1961.

Below: *Built work* – Porch, Hexenhaus, 1986. Axonometric of final version (ie. without seat aedicule being movable on diagonal track to edge of revetment). Ink on tracing paper.

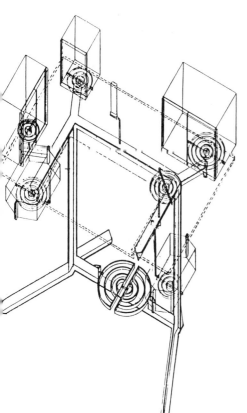

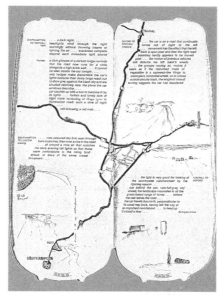

Above: *Publications – AS in DS: An Eye on the Road*, Delft University Press, 1983. Layout for double-page spread.

Left: *Furniture* – Waterlily/Fish Desk. Made by TECTA, 1986, for Milan and Cologne Furniture Exhibitions, 1986 and 87. Axonometric view from top: coloured perspex boxes over and under a neutral coloured surface (water) supported on 'waterlilies' and frame of green lustre lacquered metal.

119

# USA          Laurinda Spear *architecture*

**Biography**
Born 1951 in Rochester,
Minnesota, USA. Educated at:
Brown University, Providence,
Rhode Island, BFA, 1972;
Columbia University, New York,
MA Architecture, 1975.
Registered Architect, States of
Florida and New York; National
Council of Architectural
Registration Boards Certification.
Member of: American Institute
of Architects; Architectural Club
of Miami, co-founder; AIA
National Committee on Design;
committee 30–Council on Tall
Buildings and Urban Habitat
(UNESCO). Awards: *Progressive
Architecture* Design Award, with
Rem Koolhaas, 1975, and
citations in 1978 and 1980; New
York Society of Architects
Design Award, 1975; Rome Prize
in Architecture, 1978; South
Florida Chapter of The American
Institute of Architects, Awards
for Overseas Tower, The Palace,
and The Square at Key Biscayne,
1982 and Award for The Atlantis,
1983; *Architectural Record*,
Record Houses, for Casa los
Andes, 1986. Professional
experience: part-time faculty
member in charge of Design
Studio, University of Miami
School of Engineering and
Environmental Design, 1977,
1979; Co-founder and principal,
Arquitectonica, Coral Gables,
Florida, 1977–. Selected
exhibitions: Cooper-Hewitt
Museum, NYC, 1979; Florida
Chapter of The American
Institute of Architects, Orlando,
1979; Pennsylvania State
University, 1980; 'Young
Architects', Yale University,
1980; University of Virginia,
1981; Princeton University,
1981; Columbia University,
1981; Biennale de Paris, 1982;
Contemporary Arts Museum,
Houston, 1982; Mandeville Art
Gallery/University of California
at San Diego, 1983; Hudson
River Museum, 1983; Ewald
Scholars Symposium/Sweet Briar
College, 1983; Center For The
Fine Arts, Miami, Florida, 1984;
Fort Wayne Museum of Art,
Fort Wayne, Indiana, 1985;
Walker Art Center, Minneapolis,
Minnesota, 1985; Sarah
Campbell Blaffer Gallery,
Houston, Texas, 1985; Institute
of Contemporary Art,
Philadelphia, Pennsylvania, 1986.

The Miami based architectural firm known as
Arquitectonica (Spanish for architectural) is
renowned for producing futuristic and controversial
designs for high-rise condominiums, office buildings
and houses. Massive, multi-story buildings which
would normally possess a mechanical and
monotonous character have, in Arquitectonica's
hands, become creative experiments – incorporating
loud colours and bizarre architectural features.

Laurinda Spear and her Peruvian-born husband,
Bernardo Fort-Brescia, founded Arquitectonica in
1977, and their early buildings outraged both public
and press alike. However they quickly set the
conservative Miami establishment on its ear by
winning a cluster of prestigious design awards, and
moved into the 1980s to become one of the nation's
most successful architectural firms, with buildings
featured in design magazines all over the world.

An example of their experimental approach is their
'Atlantis' condominium in Miami: a 20-story electric-
blue apartment tower designed in 1980. A giant red
triangular prism sits on the roof, and a 37 foot cube
has been gouged out of the building's centre to create
a 'sky court', or open-air patio. Intended for use by
pleasure-seeking residents, the sky court contains a
jacuzzi, a red spiral staircase and . . . a palm tree.

Left: Bernardo Fort-Brescia
and Laurinda Spear,
Principals, Arquitectonica Inc.

Above, left and far left: Views of 'The Atlantis' condominium, Miami, Florida.

'The Atlantis is a 96 unit, 20 story condominium apartment building at the edge of Biscayne Bay in downtown Miami. The tower rests on a two storey, 200 car underground parking garage. A 37 foot cube has been removed from the building at the 12th floor creating a sky court for the building residents. This sky court contains a jacuzzi, palm tree, and red circular staircase. The Mary Tiffany Bingham Mansion originally on the site has been restored to serve as the club house for the condominium. The project also includes a lap pool, tennis and squash courts, and health club. 'This building won a *Progressive Architecture* Citation in 1980 and a South Florida Chapter of The American Institute of Architects Award in 1983.'

121

Left and below: 'The Imperial', a 162 unit, 31 storey luxury condominium building on Biscayne Bay, Miami, Florida.

# Britain          Alison de Vere *animation*

**Biography**
Born 1927 in North West India
(now Pakistan). Educated at: The
Royal Academy Schools,
London, studied painting. Then
began working in films. Design
credits include: 'Down a Long
Way' and 'Animal, Vegetable,
Mineral' for Halas and Batchelor;
'A History of Shaving' for World
Wide Pictures; and feature film
titles for Trickfilms, including
those for 'A Last Valley',
directed by James Clavell.
Backgrounds Supervisor on 'The
Yellow Submarine' for TVC.
Designed, directed and animated
'False Friends' for Interfilm.
This twelve minute piece on
opium smoking was made for the
World Health Organisation, and
won the Gold Award for British
Industrial and Scientific Films in
1968. 'Cafe Bar' (five and a half
minutes) won a Special Jury
Award at the Annecy Festival in
1975; 'Mr Pascal' won a Grand
Prix at Annecy in 1979. Both of
these films have been widely
distributed. In 1983 she made
'Silas Marner', a twenty-eight
minute TV Feature for Channel
Four, produced by Interama. In
1984 she commenced planning
and designing 'The Black Dog',
which won Best TV Film Prize
and Critics Prize at Annecy,
1987.

Alison de Vere is one of the most internationally-respected animated film-makers in Britain. She has produced a substantial body of commercial work over the years and, alongside that, a number of personal (non-commercial) projects which have made significant steps forward in conveying narrative without the use of words. These include: 'Cafe Bar', winner of the Special Jury Award at the Annecy Festival in 1975; 'Mr Pascal' – Grand Prix, Annecy 1979; and 'The Black Dog' – Best TV Film Prize and Critics Prize, Annecy 1987.

The stills shown here are from 'The Black Dog', an 18-minute film for Channel Four which de Vere began planning and designing in 1984, and which will be screened in 1988.

de Vere writes:

'I make films with drawings, ideally if possible to my own stories, and preferably without words. My goal is to entertain as many people as possible, because for me that is what cinema and television are about: All true entertainment in my view is based on real and lively ideas, and is a way through to reaching many different levels of understanding in an audience.

'By means of humour, of surprise, of curiosity, an audience may be stimulated at times to an unfamiliar thought. A prejudice may be broken, a fixed idea could maybe come a little adrift. Because gesture is understood all over the world, I can reach people whose language I cannot speak in any other way.

'But to master gesture with the drawn image, and to present it in the correct timing – for film is totally dependent on time, or should I call it sequence experienced in time? – that is the trick, the whole trick perhaps of film which uses the figurative image. And I need the figurative image, for my stories must engage the emotions of the audience, as intimately as their own dreams.'

Right: Stills from 'The Black Dog', an 18 minute film for Channel Four Television, designed and directed by Alison de Vere in 1987, to be screened in 1988.

# Lella Vignelli *architecture and design*

**Biography**
Born in Udine, Italy. Educated at: the School of Architecture, University of Venice, BA Architecture. Became registered architect in Milan in 1962. Received a tuition fellowship at the School of Architecture, Massachusetts Institute of Technology, USA, 1958. Joined Skidmore, Owings & Merrill, Chicago, as junior designer in the Interiors Department, 1959. Established, with her husband Massimo, the Lella and Massimo Office of Design and Architecture in Milan, 1960: Lella Vignelli specialized in interiors, furniture, products, and exhibition design, working on projects for major European companies and institutions. Vignelli Associates established in New York, 1971, with Lella Vignelli as President of Vignelli Designs, the branch of their organization involved in product and furniture design. Awards include: Industrial Arts Medal by the American Institute of Architects, 1973; Honorary Doctorate from the Parsons School of Design; Gold Medal from the American Institute of Graphic Arts, 1983. The Vignellis have been the subject of two film documentaries on their design, broadcast internationally. Projects conducted in both the USA and Europe include: Corporate Identity Programs; Graphics Programs; Architectural Graphics; Transportation Graphics; Book Design; Periodical Design; Packaging Design; Furniture and Product Design; Interior Design (showrooms, stores and offices); Exhibition, Museum and Trade Show Design.

Vignelli Associates, a highly successful design firm in New York, was founded in 1971 by the husband-and-wife team of Massimo and Lella Vignelli. The impact of the Vignellis on the American design scene over the past 20 years has been significant. From graphics to household objects, the Vignellis are regarded as having introduced European fashion and taste to America. But far more than that, they have succeeded in combining the European tradition of design diversification, experimentation, and elegance achieved through economy of means, with the heavily commercial, extravagance-prone, conservative establishment of American industry.

The Vignellis were both born and educated in Italy; they were married in 1958, studied in America for a short time, then established their first office of Design and Architecture in Milan. They returned to America in 1965 and, with other designers, co-founded an international office – the renowned Unimark – which crashed after a period of over-expansion.

Then Vignelli Associates came into being. Lella handles the 3D side of the work (product and furniture design); Massimo concentrates on the 2D (graphic design); together they design just about *everything* . . . Their firm commands an extremely broad range of projects: corporate identity and graphic design programmes; architectural and transportation graphics (including the New York subway map); books, magazines and newspapers; packaging; exhibition and interior design; furniture and product design. The Vignellis have had their work exhibited and published throughout the world, have received many design awards, and have lectured internationally. The Vignellis and their work have also been the subject of two feature-length television programmes which have been broadcast internationally.

Lella Vignelli received a degree in architecture from the University of Venice, and became a registered architect in Milan in 1962. According to Lella Vignelli, architectural training in Italy is very broad in scope and normally encompasses many areas of design, including courses in furniture design, product design and even stage design. Consequently she views design as a 'totality of activities', and feels that specialisation within the design field is a very limiting thing. She also maintains it is important, creatively, to work in a variety of materials, so that techniques and processes can be pushed to the limits.

Lella Vignelli is President of Vignelli Designs, the branch of the Vignelli organisation involved in product and furniture design. Over the years she has specialised in interiors, furniture, products, and exhibition design, working on projects for major European companies and institutions.

Above: Silver pitcher for San Lorenzo, Italy, 1971.

Left: 'Tara' table for Rosenthal, 1980.

Lella Vignelli

Right: 'Circolo' furniture for
Sunar, 1979.

127

Above: Office for Vignelli
Associates, 1986; 'Saratoga'
sofa for Poltronova
International, 1964;
'Torciera' lamps for
Casigliani, Italy, 1985.

Right: Office for Vignelli
Associates, 1986; 'Mesa'
table for Casigliani, Italy,
1986.

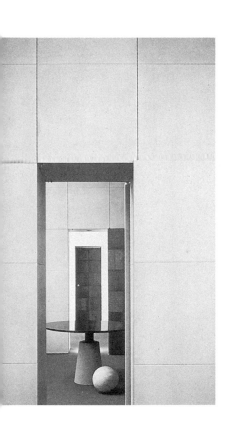

Right: Interior of St Peter's
Church, New York City,
1976–77

# Italy

# Nanda Vigo *architecture, design and environmental art*

**Biography**
Born in Milan, Italy. Educated at: Polytechnic in Lausanne. She opened her own atelier in Milan, 1959, and began to exhibit her work in galleries and museums in Europe. In the 1960s she built upon her experience as an architect and designer, to formulate a cronotopical theory of space and time. Since then, she has been constantly involved in advanced aesthetical research with Zero Group, Aktuel Group and Light and Bewegung. She has collaborated with Gio Ponti, Lucio Fontana and Piero Manzoni. Her many exhibitions include: Milan Triennale, 1964; Milan Triennale, 1973; Venice Biennale, 1982. Awards: New York Award for Industrial Design, 1971 (for Lampada Golden Gate); St. Gobain Award for Industrial Design in Milan. She still lives and works in Milan.

Initially trained as an architect and designer, Nanda Vigo developed her work in a totally unique direction, encompassing art, design, architecture and environmental projects.

She established her studio in Milan in 1959. In the 1960s she formulated a chronotopical theory (space-time) which was highly original, and an innovation for the art world at that time. Since then she has been constantly involved in the most advanced research into aesthetics, exploring the possibilities of sensorial stimuli obtained by the use of industrial materials such as glass, mirrors and neon lights. Her broad range of experience has included the creation of cronotopical objects and environments, light projects, mirror-pyramids, photography and video projects, and art installations.

Vigo has collaborated with Gio Ponti, Lucio Fontana and Piero Manzoni; and has participated in over 400 personal and group exhibitions in museums and galleries in Italy and Europe.

Right: Nanda Vigo

Left: 'Iceberg' lamp, 1969,
Arredoluce.

Brindisi Museum and private
house, Lido di Spina,
Ferrara, 1967–71.

Right: Exterior view.

Far right: Interior view.

Brindisi Museum and private
house, Lido di Spina,
Ferrara, 1967–71.

Left: Atrium/hall.

Far left: Exterior view.

Light  Track

Light  is the way of the stars
Light  is the cosmogonic alphabet
        for reading the galaxies
Light  is the infinite spaces
        of the chakra, the mind and the heart
Light  is the refractions of mirrors
        reflecting labyrinthine systems
        of light to be lost and found
Light  is the earth, mother, in the square, perfect
Light  at the centre of Khufu
Light  is the swastika of Ra's rays
        builder of life and death
        in the chronotypical light wheel
        of a becoming light

Nanda Vigo 1983

Above: 'Golden Gate' lamp,
1968, Arredoluce.

Right: Chairs and table,
glass/mirror, 1968, FAI
International, Top
Collections.

132

133

# Lorraine Wild *graphic design history, education and practice*

**Biography**

Born 1953 in Windsor, Ontario, Canada. Educated at: Cranbrook Academy of Art, USA, BFA in Graphic Design, 1975; Yale University, USA, MFA in Graphic Design, 1982. Director, Program in Visual Communication, California Institute of the Arts, 1985–. Freelance graphic design, 1978–. Clients include: Architectural Association, London; The Getty Center for the History of Art and the Humanities, Santa Monica; the Museum of Contemporary Art, Los Angeles; and many others. Has lectured on the history of graphic design at the Cooper-Hewitt Museum, Cranbrook Academy of Art, and other institutions. Publications: 'Michigan Design to 1967', *Design in Michigan 1967–1977;* 'Some posters on a theme of architecture', *Skyline,* March 1980; 'Constructivist Film Posters', *Express,* Dec 1980; 'Talk is not enough for design history', *Industrial Design,* Sept 1981; 'Exploring the roots of American Graphics', *Industrial Design,* Vol 30 No 1, Jan–Feb 1983; 'Modern American Graphics II: the birth of the profession', *Industrial Design,* Vol 30 No 4, July–Aug 1983; 'More than a few questions about graphic design education', *The Design Journal,* Vol 1 No 2, Society of Typographic Arts, Chicago, 1983; 'The Plastic Goblet', *Icographic,* Vol 11/12, July 1983, pp13–14; 'Art and design: lovers or just good friends', *AIGA Journal of Graphic Design,* Vol 5 No 2, 1987. Awards and grants: Type Directors Club, 1977; Society of Publication Designers, 1977; Design Michigan, 1977; Publication Award, Western Association of Art Museums, 1979; College and University Designers Association, 1979; Ford Foundation Project Grant, 1980; Association of American Publishers, 1982; AIGA Graphic Design USA, 1982, 1983. Permanent resident of USA.

Lorraine Wild writes from California:

'Since 1985 I have been splitting my time between being a freelance graphic designer and directing the program in Visual Communication at the California Institute of the Arts. I have a somewhat gypsy-like personal history; I am Canadian-born, then raised in Detroit, Michigan; I attended the Cranbrook Academy of Arts as an undergraduate graphic design major from 1973–75 (as Mike and Kathy McCoy were just beginning to develop their interdisciplinary design program there). I should state right away that the McCoys and another designer from Detroit, Edward Fella, were major influences from early on; their relentless interest in both theoretical and formal issues in design provided a wonderful example of just how rich the "culture" of design was, and I was hooked . . . At Cranbrook there was a terrific library with a lot of historical material, and again under the encouragement of the McCoys I began to use graphic design history as a resource for my own work. After graduation I worked in Detroit until 1977; then I moved to New York City where I worked for Vignelli Associates and also as a freelance designer. At Vignelli Associates I did a lot of work for the (now defunct) Institute for Architecture and Urban Studies, which brought me into contact with another incredibly energetic intellectual scene. The Institute's lectures and critiques and publishing projects impressed and inspired me to attempt to develop work that had both a formal and a critical depth to it. That sent me back to school – in 1980 I entered the graduate program in graphic design at the Yale School of Art.

'Shortly after graduating I moved to Texas to begin teaching in the architecture program in the University of Houston. While I was there I became the art director for a local design tabloid *Cite*, and I also embarked on the design of two important publications; the first was *Mask of Medusa*, a book on the work of the American architect John Hejduk (published by Rizzoli); the second was *Chamber Works*, a folio by the architect Daniel Libeskind (published by the Architectural Association, London). In both cases the books presented unique opportunities to experiment with typography and layout as expressions of (quite complex) content.

'In 1985 I accepted my current job at CalArts. The program has about 70 students (approx. 15 graduate students, the rest undergrads) and 10 faculty members. My position gives me the opportunity to shape the direction of the program in conjunction with the faculty – we really are free to design the program as we see fit. I am particularly interested in trying to develop a program that provides, but also transcends, professional training. I think the most interesting work going on right now is marginal work: design by non-designers, art, photography, etc. Also, Postmodernist theory and recent design history are very important to include in the curriculum – we are trying to train designers who will be literate and able to understand the wider social and cultural context that their work fits into. I am also interested in developing work that is not dependent on the traditional designer-client relationship. We ask our students to become entrepreneurial – because the way that the technology is developing it is going to take less and less, for example, to publish or produce ideas without needing someone else's ideas or capital. I think we are in a conservative period in design, partially because all of society's that way, but also because there has been a lot of doubt about how the new technologies are going to change things – but students are excited and want to move forward, and it's a challenging time to be teaching for that reason.

'You *(the author)* ask, as only another woman would, about support for women in the discipline and balancing work and life. Los Angeles is an interesting place in this aspect because it seems to be one of the few places where there are many women in charge of their own offices (Deborah Sussman, April Greiman, Sheila de Bretteville, and many others come immediately to mind). I think this is because LA is notoriously low on tradition and there has been the "space" and perhaps just a smidgen less of ingrained sexism to do battle with. Certainly the climate is nothing like New York where men still seem to run *everything*. CalArts is also incredibly fair – the Provost and half of the Deans are women and the student population is balanced as well. This is not to say that CalArts is an unblemished paradise – we have our institutionalized neuroses, just like every other art school. But a very interesting community is messing around with ideas and technology that challenge the old hierarchical ways that design is produced. The work looks different. Every critique is an adventure – which is what design is supposed to be like, anyway, isn't it?'

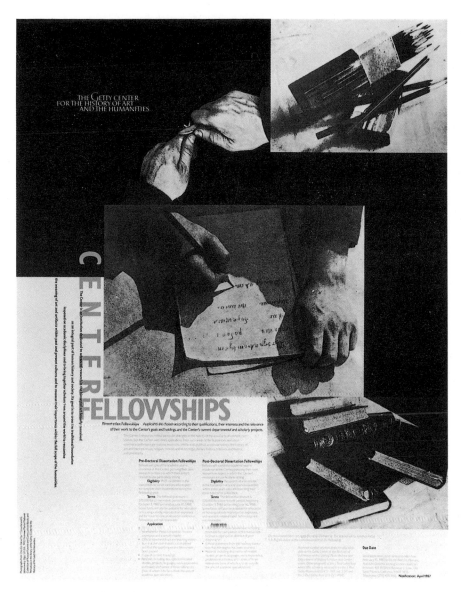

Poster, The Getty Center for
the History of Art and the
Humanities, Los Angeles,
1987.

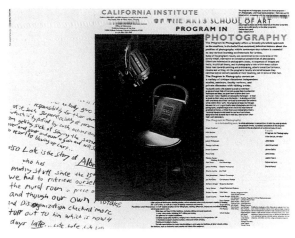

Poster for lecture series,
University of Houston.

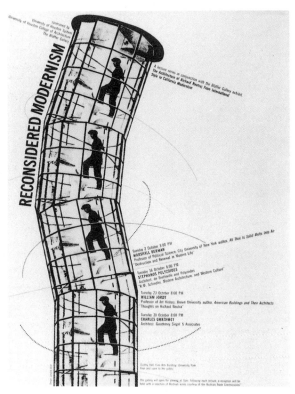

Poster, California Institute of
the Arts.

Lorraine Wild

135

# Italy

# Lynne Wilson *furniture design and printed textiles*

**Biography**
Born 1952 in Epsom, England.
Educated at: Kingston
Polytechnic, England, BA in
Furniture Design, 1975; Royal
College of Art, London, MA in
Design, 1979. Awarded the
Sanderson Scholarship in 1978.
Design apprentice for three
months in Centro Design
Prototipo at Cassina S.p.A.
Meda, Italy. Worked with Mario
Bellini on projects for Rosenthal,
Germany, and Cleto Munari,
Italy, 1979–80. Began working as
a freelance designer within the
Italian furniture industry, 1982;
collaborated with Mobilia Italia
S.r.L. on first commercial
product 'Lotto', presented at

Salone del Mobile in Milan,
1983; began working with Centro
Design e Comunicazione S.r.L.
Milan, on furnishing textiles,
1984; designed textile collection
'Oltre il Giardino' for Assia
S.p.A. Briosco, 1985; prototype
'Felice' presented at Salone del
Mobile, Milan, 1985; 'Toba', a
knock-down table designed at the
Royal College of Art in 1979,
goes into production for the
company 'Gemini' in Udine,
Italy, 1985; textile collection 'Il
Risveglio' for Assia S.p.A.
Briosco, shown at textile fair
Star, Milan, 1986; collection of
curtains 'Paradiso ritrovato' for
Fanair S.r.L. Florence presented
at Incontri Venezia, 1987.

Right: Samurai chair,
structure in sycamore, back
in curved galvanised sheet
metal – held together by
leather thong, base covered
in linoleum, 1979.

Lynne Wilson worked internationally with her
parents E + EG Wilson in the field of exhibition
design (museums, trade fairs etc) before entering the
Royal College of Art in 1976 to study furniture
design. While at the RCA she was awarded the
Sanderson Scholarship which allowed her to travel to
South East Asia, researching into the decorative arts.
She received her Masters degree in 1979, arrived in
Milan the same year and has since then worked as a
freelance designer within the Italian furniture
industry. Her commercial products include the
furniture designs 'Lotto' and 'Felice', presented at
the Salone del Mobile in Milan in 1983 and 1985
respectively; and from 1985–87, textile collections
created in collaboration with Centro Design e
Comunicazione for Assia SpA Briosco and Fanair Srl
Florence.

Wilson provides a glimpse of her design approach
and methods through a collection of notes, sketches,
and prototypes.

Left: Lynne Wilson

'I have always had a
strong attraction to
artifacts of those cultures
which we term primitive,
characterised as they are
by their complete
simplicity of approach to
subject and technique. At
the same time I have been
excited by the possibilities
offered by modern
technology, in both
technique and materials,
for the resolution of
design problems. It is the
relationship between
these apparently diverse
areas of interest that
significantly influence my
work.

'In textiles I enjoy the
medium of mechanical
techniques to give form to
my idea. I like the
expression of an idea
interpreted through
artificial means, where
accidental qualities play
an important role. From
Matisse I learnt of the
richness of colours in the
textured depths of his
tempura paper cut outs,
from Max Ernst his
frottage techniques.

'In textiles, as in
furniture, the technique is
integral to the design.
'When designing an
object I look for that
quality which is innate to

136

the materials employed and the way in which they are used in the structure of an object. It is important that the process of manufacture of an object relates directly to the overall 'feel' of the form: so that each component part complements the whole, yet at the same time performs its precise function within the structure, so that one can always sense a unity and order within the form of an object.

'There is also a strong historical background influence to my work; "Lotto" was derived from 19th Century designs of deckchairs found on cruise ships manufactured by C + R Light in 1881.

'In Italy I have found an ideal working relationship. In the development of a product, the component parts are farmed out to different industries so I have gained a wider working experience of manufacturing techniques. Here, I don't feel restricted to my principle discipline of furniture design and can move freely into the field of printed textiles.'

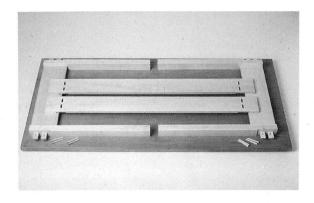 

Above and right: 'Toba' knock-down table, structure in sycamore, zinc top, 1979; prod. Gemini/Italy, 1985.

Below: Olmo Group, seat in laminate plywood, structure in epoxy coated metal tube, woven plastic back, 1979.

Right and far right: 'Lotto' armchair, 1985.
Extreme right: Historical reference for 'Lotto', 1982.

'"Lotto" was designed to be simple and easy to manufacture in component parts. The chair is comprised of two interlocking structures. A seat with legs and a back with legs join together to form a chair. One is fat and one is thin. One has narrow round legs, the other wide oval legs. The back can be made taller by a detachable head rest, and a "pouff" brought close for one's feet. Two of them join together to form a sofa. Alternatively, a raised table can sit between them holding them apart.'

Below: Drawing for 'Felice'.

1235

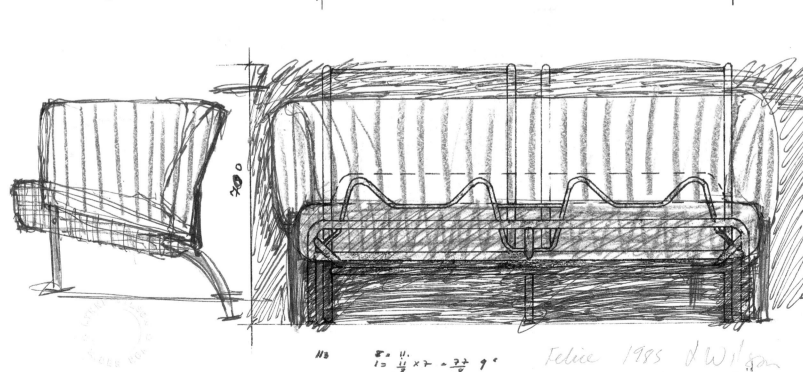

Felice 1985 dWilson

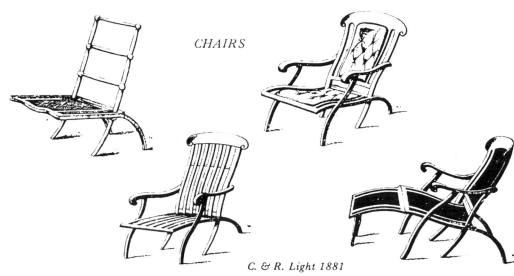

*CHAIRS*

*C. & R. Light 1881*

Left: Prototype for 'Felice' two-seater sofa, structure in metal tube with paint finish, upholstery in polyurethane – with dacron covering and cotton removable covers, Centro Design e Comunicazione, Italy, 1985.

139

Right: Still from the animated television commercial 'Fleetwood Mac' (Tango in the Night) for WEA Records, prod. Metcalf & Mills. This particular image was used by WEA for fly-posters.

Far right: Still from the anti-nuclear film 'The Doomsday Clock' (with Jonathan Hodgson), for the United Nations, prod. Unicorn Productions.
The still shows the crux of the film: two arguing world leaders are warned by two skeletons pointing at a clock with its hands frozen at midnight (ie. nuclear war imminent). The skeletons appear throughout the film, hovering in the air over people and events, as a symbol of both collective and individual fear of nuclear catastrophe. The leaders and background were drawn by Jonathan Hodgson, the skeletons by Susan Young.

Below: Stills from the film 'Carnival', 1985.

# Photographic credits

**p9**: Ian Loveday; **p18**: *above left*, Aldo Ballo, Milan; **p19**: *top*, Giovanna Nuvoletti; *bottom*, Carla De Benedetti; **p21**: *left centre*, Brad Fowler; *right top*, Dennis M Swanson; **p22**: *bottom*, Linda Okamura Photography, Los Angeles, CA; **p23**: *top and bottom*, Dennis M Swanson; **p30–31**: Richard Rose, Marc Treib; **p32**: *left*, Robert Mapplethorpe; **p33**: *top*, Marie Cosindas; **p34**: MIT Visible Language Workshop; **p37**: *top*, Steve Speller, London; **p45**: *top and centre left*, Roy Wales, London; **p48–49**: *bottom*, Walker Art Center and Massachusetts Institute of Technology; **p57**: *top*, Masao Arai; *bottom*, Masao Arai, © Shinkenchiku; **p58**: *top and bottom*, Horishi Ueda, © Shinkenchiku; **p60**: *bottom right*, agency Collett Dickenson Pearce, client Radio Rentals; **p61**: *bottom centre*, prod. Kirkwood and Partners; **p71**: *centre*, Nina Hauser Swanson, Bloomfield Hills, MI; **p73**: *top*, Tim Street-Porter; **p74**: *below left*, Steve Speller, London; **p80**: Bertrand Prévost, Paris; **p84**: Financial Times Photography, London; **p85**: *top left*, P K Childs; *top right*, British Rail; *centre left and right*, *bottom left and right*, P K Childs; **p86**: *above right and below right*, Renzo Chiesa, Milan; **p95**: Dudley Reed, London; **p111**: *bottom*, Felix Fonteyn, London; **p112**: *top right*, Vickers-Armstrongs (Aircraft) Ltd, Surrey, England; **p114**: Andreas Sterzing, © SITE Projects Inc; **p115–117**: Oberto Gilli and Andreas Sterzing, © SITE Projects Inc 1985; **p130**: *bottom left*, Maria Mulas, Milan; *top right*, Arredoluce; **p130–131**: *bottom centre*, Aldo Ballo, Milan; **p131**: *bottom, top left and top right*, Aldo Ballo, Milan; **p132**: *left*, Ugo Hulas; **p132–133**: *centre*, Aldo Ballo, Milan; **p133**; *right*, Aldo Ballo, Milan; **p139**: *bottom*, Franco Ziglioli, Italy.